GULL STONES AND CUCKOOS

First published in 2016
By Unthank Books
www.unthankbooks.com

Book production & design by Silly Spaceman
Printed in England by Lightning Source

A CIP record for this book is available from the British Library

The accounts written here are the recollections of our writers who retain individual copyright on their words. In one sensitive account, names have been changed to protect the anonymity of the persons involved.

ISBN 978-1-910061-41-1

Edited by Lynne Bryan and Belona Greenwood
Cover art by Kate Munro
Illustrations by Rose Cowan

CONTENTS

Country Life

Introduction

Belona Greenwood

This book is the result of an idle half-thought in a second hand bookshop. On a shelf labelled country life, there was nothing either written by women or about women's lives in the countryside. I wondered even more idly what had been written about women's lives in a rural environment since the famous Paston Letters, what would women write about living in rural Norfolk today? I talked it over with my Co-organiser of Words and Women, Lynne Bryan, and the project began to form. Next stop was Anna Brett of Create Projects who with her customary clarity of thinking and organisational skills formed the spine of the project. Norfolk Library and Information Service became our partners, and Arts Council England generously supported 'Rural Writes'.

Anna and the library service identified three areas of comparative rural or coastal isolation: Gorleston and The Magdalen Estate, Watton and Swaffham. We wanted to recruit women from all ages, backgrounds and ethnicities, and especially hoped to attract the hard-to-reach, mothers and women who lived in isolation. We wanted to bring in those who didn't consider themselves to be writers, the beginners who wanted to have a go and had a story they wanted to share.

There were to be 10 weeks of free life-writing workshops held in the local libraries of our target areas. Norfolk Library Service offered digital support, computers, and plenty of tea and biscuits. We set up a blog. I was joined by poet Heidi Williamson, a local girl who grew up in Swaffham, who would help the women to explore life-writing through poetry.

The women who joined us were strangers to each other, the youngest 25, the oldest 96. They came from all social backgrounds, and different ethnicities; we had women from the Philippines, Lithuania, Romania and America, as well as of Jamaican and Nigerian origin. Some of our women were incomers from Manchester, Liverpool and Brixton, others were Norfolk born and bred. All our women led busy lives, were often carers of children or the ill and elderly, and yet managed to fit in a phenomenal amount of homework.

It hasn't been easy. As the women explored and wrote about their lives, there were often tears – I think the record was five women in tears in Swaffham one Friday morning - but there has been an awful lot of laughter, generosity and support for each other. Sometimes just a bit too much natter but all the women have had to robustly take on writing, criticism and editing which would be daunting even for professional writers. For me, all the women who have taken part are brave. This process has been about authenticity, exposing memory, unlocking the personal and true, and the groups became trusted spaces where women could share freely. We all learnt from each other and compassion, empathy and understanding have grown, friendships formed. All of the groups have elected to continue meeting, writing and blogging. There is a sense of community within the groups in the individual areas and between the groups.

This book is full of the telling detail of lives rooted in place, about relationships with memory and time, family, people and place. What comes through is a love of Norfolk, but also a clear eye on what is changing and what it means to live a rural life today.

There are so many people to thank in the making of this project and this book: All the women who joined us and worked so hard.

Jan Holden, Head of Norfolk Library and Information Service, the community librarians and managers who hosted us at Gorleston, Watton and Swaffham, Kathryn Jennings and Rachel Houghton. Arts Council England: without their generous support this project would not exist. Anna Brett of Create Projects for her marvellous organisational skills, calm efficiency and personal support, Norfolk County Council, Heidi Williamson for her inspirational poetry sessions, Rose Cowan for her brilliant illustrations, Kate Munro for her wonderful cover design, Unthank Books, Ashley Stokes, Tom Collin and everyone involved in the production of this book. And finally, Co-organiser of Words and Women, Lynne Bryan whose clarity, skillful editing and stoicism are unrivalled.

Thank you.

Belona Greenwood, Founder and Co-organiser, Words and Women, August, 2016.

Preface

Jan Holden

Norfolk Library and Information Service with libraries situated at the heart of 47 communities across Norfolk has been excited to be part of Rural Writes.

Congratulations to all the authors that have taken part. An idle half hour in a second-hand book shop has resulted in many hours of creativity in libraries in Gorleston, Swaffham, and Watton supported by our generous funders Arts Council England and brilliantly led by Belona and Heidi.

Local libraries are places to connect and create and where local talent can be incubated. Rural Writes is an example of how libraries and writers can support one another.

Libraries in Norfolk are vibrant, accessible and exciting places where words come alive in all kinds of different ways. The brave women involved in the project have all gone out of their comfort zones to create a community of writers that will last beyond the life of this project, a community of women that will continue to share experiences and write about them in a supportive environment, their local library.

Jan Holden, Head of Service, Norfolk Library and Information Service, August, 2016.

Wildlife

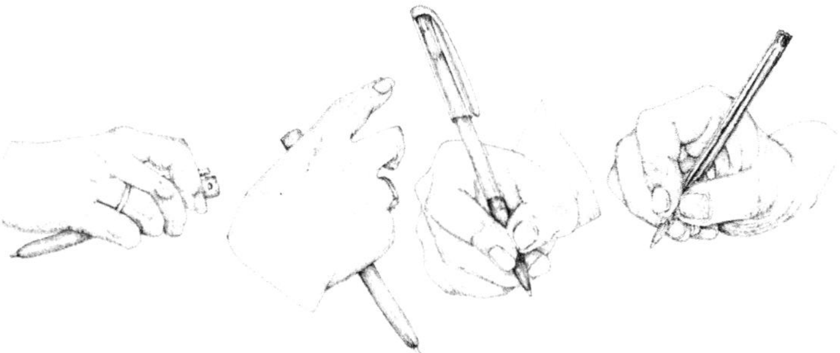

Dawn

Gill Ashton

The first train stops and waits for the signal. Nothing. The train waits but the signal still says no; the man in box must have gone to sleep. The diesel engine chugs and rumbles waiting for the signal to change. Still nothing. So the train driver sounds the horn, loud, sharp like a knife, disturbing the rooks from their nightly sleep. A black cloud goes up and round chattering, unsure where to go. The signal changes with a loud clunk, and the diesel roars down the track, slowly getting fainter as it goes, further and further until the silence returns.

The east sky now shows the first faint orange glow of the still hidden morning sun. Dew forms on the grass, wet and cold, covering the spider's delicate silk webs with shimmering diamond droplets. In the distance a black bird chirps ready to announce the dawn, and slowly a chorus works across the land.

Beachamwell

Leah Spencer

An island surrounded by fields.
Ploughed, harrowed, seeded, harvested,
the once hedge-bound pools of land
swollen into seas and oceans.
Combines ride the swell of furrowed acres.

Spring: Long Drove

We are newcomers navigating village backwaters,
when we first enter this hedge-bound byway
to follow the winter-cut tractor ridges up the hill
and crest it with anticipation in our steps.

In the shallow drilled field of green corn to the east
the solitary pillbox stands, a reminder of war
that saw searchlights placed on this ancient way,
their night beams slicing the sky.
To the west the deep potato field furrows flow on
down to the airfield, to the hidden cold war bunker.

We are sailing headstrong into the future
as spent blackthorn blossom withers,
and bursting hawthorn sweetens the hedgerows.
Buds are swelling as we race through the waves of
white foam, the delicate spray of Queen Anne's Lace.
Fieldfares and redwings have flown, it is the time
for greenfinch, skylark, yellow hammer and linnet.

Stand still, breathe softly, watch in wonder as ahead
a hare bounds down to Devil's Dyke, site of forgotten
Celtic magic and Saxon safety.
He stops, as we do, a snapshot in bated breath.

Summer: Smeeth's Field

This ancient outcrop is never ploughed -
a lonely reminder of ancient, rabbit-rich heath days;
thousands within golden, gorse-crested battlements.
Now only traces of those broken banks remain
among the few solitary furze bush souvenirs.

Rabbits still crop the grasses, wary of buzzards' circling
or the distant call of the fox's nighttime bark.
Mole hills of golden sand mark my way
and my shoes follow the path over campion and speedwell,
plantain and wild geranium; while roots pass down
through the darkness, through tunnels and burrows,
past lost, everyday things – stone arrow head,

Roman coin, broken pot, a lover's pin.

In crossing from one string-bound gate to the other
over the old heath from Warren Barn to Warren Lodge,
I have seen my younger self, walking carefree in distant sunshine.

Autumn: Restricted Byway

There is warmth in the sun on this ageing track
and our steps are still strong as we stride to the forest edge.
Our path passes fallow fields and mixed plantations;
ash, oak and hazel leaves turn gold, as we turn grey.

Summer verges, once vibrant with bugloss and bees,
now toss their dead seed heads into the breeze.
Where white admirals gorged on bramble flowers,
ripening red-black berries glow out among the thorns.

This is the bygone way the children walked
from far flung cottages and farms in rain, wind,
snow and sun. Running, dawdling, chattering in those
far off, stone scuffing, bird-nesting, blackberry-eating
school days. Their presence whispers here still
as we talk of childhood and walk on to the forest.

Ahead, ranks of pine, deep dark impenetrable forest
and we talk of moonlit walks to hear the nightjars cry,
their long remembered sounds still haunt us as we turn for home

hands held, backs bent into the strengthening wind.

Winter: Shouldham Lane

Hedgerows are hoar frost white and our breaths cloud the air,
we are leaving our small haven for the harbour of the town.
We take a slow way, an ancient passage, from the known.
We have loosened the ties and cast ourselves adrift.

Behind us, like flotsam, the memories of our lives –
dreamlike, golden days of summer trailing in our wake
joining the jetsam of our shared sorrows – lost loves,
disappointments and the distant dreams of youth.

With one brief glimpse westward to the setting sun,
we turn to the light of a new berth dawning in the east.
Ahead, landmark church spire, water tower and turbine,
skyline silhouettes fixing our position as light fades.

Curious But Not Cunning

Maxine Robertson

Dusk is beginning to swallow up the daylight as we arrive back at the house. When prompted, Alfie robotically lifts each muddy paw, one at a time, so that I can wipe them on his towel, before allowing him indoors. As I unclip his lead I'm gripped by an eerie sense of someone watching us. For a few seconds in the disappearing light, I feel frightened by the uncertainty of who else may be there. I glance over my shoulder to the lawn. A rusty brown creature sits motionless about six feet away from us. The stranger's triangular be-whiskered face and black glossy snout go with his triangular black-tipped ears. His bushy tail resembles my sheepskin duster, an obvious clue to his identity. When I realise who he is, I am surprised there is nothing aggressive about his posture. I expect him to look evil, cunning and not curious as he does. Our eyes connect and we hold one another's gaze for a few moments, mesmerised, before he saunters across the garden and disappears into the hedge.

A short while later, I return to my garden to feed my cats and am startled by the sight of my rusty visitor lying in a cat bed at the back of my garage. The image of him lying there, peering at me, again feels unreal. As we stare, it is as though we are tuned into one another. His youthfulness suggests he may be one of the cubs I'd admired earlier in the year. If so, I know where he lives but I won't tell.

I wonder if he is expecting something from me, food perhaps. I think of the chef Gordon Ramsay who encouraged a vulpine visitor into his garden by offering gourmet titbits. For a moment I'm tempted but decide against it. He's a wild animal and the surrounding fields are an abundant larder. I feel comforted knowing my ducks are locked up for the night. My five cats seem unconcerned by his presence yet I have often read that his kind like to attack felines. Perhaps he's different.

Despite several sightings, my ducks remain intact and my cats and dogs don't get mange!

How blessed I feel to have been so close to such a handsome creature. Then my head fills with whispers telling me how evil and crafty his type are. 'He's no good. You wait until he's visited your chickens, then you'll change your mind. He needs the bullet.' These voices belong to others and are not my own.

I wonder if I should feel guilty or disloyal for having admired my visitor? Should I be thinking of the impact he might have on farm livestock? I feel sympathy for farmers who lose their lambs to his sort but is he always our enemy? My emotions argue with one another. I know he isn't harmless but find it hard to see him as a pilfering villain either. I prefer to believe that wild creatures don't have a one- size personality any more than humans do. This stirs a memory of a recent report of someone being attacked by a gang of squirrels in a wood and, although I empathise with the horror of that, I can't accept all squirrels are members of a violent squad that attacks humans.

Thoughts of hunting enter my head. I don't want to kill him for 'nothing' and I don't want to kill him for 'something' either. I have had unfavourable visits from Mr Tod's companions in the past but still I can't bring myself to hurt him.

One winter's morning I was greeted by the chilling sight of the headless corpses of every one of my lumpy-beaked Muscovy ducks floating in our pond. I prefer to believe that their decapitation was due to a vixen needing to provide nourishment for her cubs, rather than that she'd killed for fun. I was bereft but if you have a young fox family to feed you can't exactly nip round to Tesco to obtain provisions. Anyway, was I partially to blame for having left the Muscovy gang out at night? In an attempt to discourage future visits, I laced the boundaries of my garden with a deterrent containing lion dung. Of course, it didn't work.

Then, I was woken early one summer's morning by a commotion under my bedroom window. Instinct drove me to leap out of bed. As I glanced through the chink in the curtains, still struggling to open my eyes, I saw an anorexic- looking fox standing on the lawn below my window with its jaws clamped tightly round the head of Dotty Duck, the matriarch of the new Muscovy clan. Through the now opened window, I hollered at the robber which thankfully resulted in him releasing Dotty from his vice-like jaws and scarpering across the garden. Apart from a few blood spots and a short spell of shock, Dotty was fine.

Although my personal journey with foxes has been bumpy, they continue to arouse my curiosity and are still creatures I prize. Your journey may be different and I respect that.

Down Loch Lane

M.C. Gardner

Past the enclosed waters of Loch Neaton encircled by a dense scaffold of vegetation, and I am in the field of barley. The fields were vast. They are smaller now. Impressive architect-designed houses, with landscaped bijou gardens, have gnawed at the earth.

In the distance, the milky sight of the fog hinders my view.

As I walk on with my dogs, the wildlife shuffles from its hiding places. Red poppies scramble for spaces between the field and the hedges. Fumes break loose from the soil. The air turns and tosses. A hare jumps from the undergrowth and hides in the barley. Yellow gorse embroiders the hedges.

I walk by the side of the field with the dogs far ahead. I whistle the dogs and they bark in return.

I shall cross the ford at the end of the path and be in the woodland. Spider webs net the trees in the fresh light. The dogs begin to wail, and I break into a run.

I freeze. I stand. I stand there. I stare. A rope is taut between the boundary's two oak trees and the path. A shabby garment waves from side to side. A body tremours in the breeze. I get closer. I stare. I recognize him. The old farmer. Last weekend, I bought goose eggs from him. He told me that he had lost his wife before Christmas. He felt trapped in loneliness. I half-listened when he told me it was the end of the line for him. Dry-mouthed he mumbled that his tenancy was to end that month, and that he was about to be evicted. The land had been sold for new houses.

The mist loiters as I search for my mobile. Above, cranes hover in the sea of blue. I get the whistle out. Three distinctive shapes are gaining ground, tails wagging, and a duckling in each mouth.

Fields

Gill Ashton

Muddy roads, half-built walls, men in hard hats, the churning of a mixer on and on. Flashing lights of the diggers. For sale boards driven into the remains of the verge.

Where have the hares gone? No crops to hide in from predator's eyes. The blackbird sings no more, no need, no territory to protect.

The old oak still remains. Beneath it a hedgehog awakens from his winter sleep. Where will he go? We don't care. We need new homes.

Family And Friends

The Norfolk Widow

Julia Howarth

She looks out of the streaked window
No one around.
Just cold grey sea and blowing sand.

No nearby shops to hobble to,
no husband now, to tell off,
to clean the salt windows.

An old peoples' home
Suggested by helpful friends,
Clean windows, help and routine
Lifts her spirits.

She is at home, their home,

In his chair.
Feeling her bottom, warm,
warm and moulded to his shape.
She always said he had a hot bottom.
That thought brings a smile.

How she misses him.
It is lonely here,
But at least she has Tibby
And the sea is always there.

Changing, challenging, everlasting.
Bringing continuity and comfort.
And an element of danger.

Time to think, reflect and remember.
Life and sea, storms and beauty,
Love and death intertwined.

Cuckoo!

Cynthia Gallogo

Cuckoo! Cuckoo! I was woken by this mysterious sound one sunny morning. My bedside clock said it was 6 a.m. and I lazily turned around to check where the sound was coming from. Cuckoo! Cuckoo! It went on. When I looked up at the window set high in our bedroom wall, I saw a dove-sized bird resting there. It had blue-grey upper parts and some white underneath, on its chest. Briefly, I thought the bird and I exchanged a moment of meaningful eye contact. Then, it flew away.

My husband and I have lived in Gorleston for over a decade. Gorleston-on-Sea is a small town, just to the south of Great Yarmouth. It is known for its stunning sandy beach stretching into the distance below cliff gardens and a grand promenade. I feel lucky to live by the sea. On a good summer's day we go to the beach for a stroll, attend the Clifftop Festival if it is on or watch live bands at the band stand surrounded by deckchairs. Sometimes my son also goes for a dip at the children's pool with his friends. In the winter, we love to watch theatre plays at Gorleston Pavilion or eat fish and chips at the seashore.

Like me, my husband has also moved around before settling in this area. He was originally from Scotland, while I come from the Philippines. In Gorleston, we live in a 2 bedroom mid-terrace house close to St. Andrews Church. The church has a tower and a huge clock at the top. It also has a graveyard which we use as short-cut to my son's school. He attends St. Mary's and St. Peter's Catholic school. When I first moved to Gorleston, I used the church tower as a landmark to help me find my way home. On Sunday mornings I hear the church bells ringing and sometimes hear hymn singing from our garden. In the summer it is always a delight watching wedding processions thread through the churchyard filled with huge yellow, white and pink roses. In contrast I have seen several funeral services held at this Church and have said my prayers to the dead even if they're strangers to me.

On the morning I first saw the bird I took my son to school and then drove myself to work. Although I was concentrating on my driving, I could not resist thinking of the bird. Our eye-contact was unforgettable. I remembered that some people believe that birds can either bring good luck or be a bad omen. But some people say it's only crows or black birds that are a bad omen. So, I thought, it must be good luck then. I smiled and cheerfully arrived at work.

It was early summer in 2013. I can remember that it was a season with much to celebrate. Andy Murray won Wimbledon and a Brit claimed the yellow jersey in the Tour de France for the second year running. But, for most of us, the greatest reward was that Britain basked in sunshine. So many beautifully warm days and nights.

The next morning, lo and behold, I was woken by the same sound. Cuckoo, cuckoo! When I looked up, the bird was again resting on our window, looking at me. This time, it felt like she was telling me something. The sound went on for nearly 2 minutes before the bird flew away. I hurried to my son's room to ask him if he'd heard the sound, but he was still fast asleep. So I went downstairs for my morning coffee and checked our small back garden for the bird. I noticed that our neighbours' garden flowers were in full bloom. Beautiful pink dahlias, marigolds, and giant blowsy roses. It is a tradition and nearly a competition among my neighbours to have the best garden. I was busy working and juggling family life, so my garden was least of my priorities. My thoughts were interrupted by the sound of screaming seagulls flying around the big oak tree near the church, but my bird was nowhere to be seen.

On the third day, she came back again at 6 o'clock. Now I was more prepared to welcome my new friend. I smiled and said, 'Hi, I don't know your name but can I call you cuckoo?' I went on to say, 'I am very thankful and grateful for your visits. I hope that you will carry on waking me up.' Again, after an exchange of eye contact, my cuckoo flew away.

I was too rushed off my feet that day to do any research on birds. Eventually, though, I discovered from the RSPB files that there is a migratory bird called cuckoo and that they look like doves.

My research said that birds symbolize the unfolding of an event in life. Cuckoos also reflect a change in your home or family. They can also be connected to birth and fertility.

I told my family about Cuckoo, my new friend. My husband, who was then working in Angola, Africa, thought it was strange, while my young son was amused.

For nearly a month, Cuckoo visited me each morning. I found myself telling her about my family and my stressful job. Perhaps I sound strange but those brief moments had me reflecting about my life. I noticed that the glass window high on our bedroom wall looks dull from our driveway, but on a clear night sky I could see the moon and the stars through it. Before closing my eyes, I bathed in moonlight as I savoured the last tranquil minutes of the day. On a summer's day, the sun shone through it.

But summer was nearly over. I was working hard, driving long distances between Norfolk and Suffolk. My company was on the brink of collapse and my colleagues and I were determined to turn it round. My husband, who was still working in Angola, told me that his knees were playing up. My son and I were both worried and hoped he'd recuperate. The neighbouring gardens were still in full bloom, although some of the spring flowers had died.

Cuckoo! Cuckoo! Cuckoo! I was half asleep, half awake. I thought I was dreaming. But this time the sound was strangely louder. When I looked at the high window, my cuckoo had brought a friend. Both of them looked at me and, once again, we were locked in mysteriously meaningful eye-contact. I told her, 'I am pleased to see your friend.' Not long after, the cuckooing stopped and both birds flew away. I never imagined it would be the last time I would see either of them.

The next morning, I woke up at the same time. But there was no Cuckoo. I looked at the window and waited. But she never came back. I said goodbye and wished my friend the best journey.

Towards the end of that year, my husband and I, together with our son, went on holiday to Thailand. Two months later, I had a lovely surprise. I was pregnant and we were having a girl. Then I remembered Cuckoo. Perhaps this was the meaning of her visits. A new beginning.

Tears ran down my cheeks.

The Blue Scooter

Jane Rudd

Lizzie whizzed around the block on her blue scooter. She loved it so much, and there was nothing to beat going at speed and feeling the wind through her hair. She felt free and alive. She knew the rules though; her mum had told her as she left the house, 'Don't go over the road away from the block or you will go to bed early.' From where Lizzie was, spinning round and round on the pavement on her side of the road, the houses on the other side looked new and exciting.

Lizzie arrived at the back gate. She was so thirsty; she barely paused to prop the scooter against the outside wall before she ran down the path. The gate slammed behind her leaving her precious scooter completely out of sight.

Lizzie opened the door with such vigour it made her mum cross. 'I've told you not to come in the door like that – you'll have it off its hinges! For goodness sake, slow down!'

Lizzie grabbed the glass off the work top, filled it, gasping with thirst. She guzzled the water down, hanging onto the taps. Finished, she banged the glass down and skipped to the back gate, anxious to return to her scooter.

Lizzie flung open the gate. She looked left and right. There was no scooter. Devastated, she ran to the corner of the road, expecting to see a neighbourhood child waiting with her scooter, playing a joke on her, but there was no one, nothing. She ran back to her mum, crying, her red face tear-stained.

'Someone's taken my scooter,' she wept.

Her mum's tone changed instantly, 'Oh dear, love, I expect you've left it somewhere.' If this was meant to be comforting it wasn't. Taking Lizzie by the hand, Lizzie's mum led her to the back gate. They both looked out expectantly. No scooter. 'Perhaps someone's borrowed it,' her mum said encouragingly. 'Let's hope it will turn up.'

Back in the kitchen, Lizzie's mum sat Lizzie in a chair and gave her a rare chocolate biscuit to pacify her.

The Girl Who Climbed Out Of A Window And Opened A Door

Jenni Jones

Before we moved to the Barrack Estate, we lived in flats near the library in Great Yarmouth. I was five, without a care in the world, under the supervision of my sister who had the care of all of us younger ones, when we played out front. I was completely obsessed with Mr Blobby. I had Mr Blobby roller skates. One day I was skating out front when a stone wedged into the wheels and I took a tumble. I suffered a serious break on my left arm, my bone was pushing out. My big sister came to the rescue and ran to our block to the very top where we lived. My dad rushed down to me and put wooden blocks around my arm in a sort of splint. After the operation I was told his action had saved my arm from being amputated.

Happy times.

After that we moved to the Barrack Estate. I was six and everything was lovely for another year or so. Every other Saturday me and my siblings used to go to my Nan and Grandad's house for the day. They lived on the same street as us.

From there, in the summer months, we would visit the pleasure beach. We would arrive before the gates opened and stay until they closed. We only popped home for our tea. They were days when we could be free, like proper children. The thing is there were none of life's worries on the pleasure beach. For a start it was full of colour and sound – it was as if the pleasure beach was determined to enjoy itself – with the Rollercoaster and Skydrop or the Haunted Hotel. We used to go on the big rides as well as the small ones.

On the smaller rides, we pretended we were racing on giant snails and carousel horses. We cheered each other on although we never caught each other up and never could. At that time, me and my sister were still good friends.

If it was wet, we played on the 2p pushers; the prize was a teddy holding a £2 coin and during that last summer we won lots of them. We were wild with freedom, and used to sit in the last rollercoaster car, backwards, which was very scary going down the hills. Twice I hit my mouth on the bar and pushed my teeth through my bottom lip and had to visit the first aid room. Another time, my sister chipped her tooth on the water flume – which we always laughed about.

If we weren't at the pleasure beach we would be down the play-park with friends. I was always on the swings and slide, or wriggling across the monkey bars. If there was a lot of us, we would play bulldog. They seem gilded, those times. We spent hours in a broken-down car, in the garden. My uncle often fixed cars and it was one of his. We pretended to change gears and push the pedals imagining all the places we wanted to visit.

We always had arts and crafts, chalks, glue, glitter, card and pencils on rainy days and spent hours sitting up the table, crafting away, listening to the rain.

That was then.

Christmas Eve we had a family tradition. We had baths, wore new pyjamas and slept in freshly-washed bedding ready for Santa to visit. We always went to bed early and could never sleep. The excitement was overwhelming. In the morning, us three girls who shared a bedroom at the front of the house would take it in turns to ask our parents if we could get up. When Mum and Dad were still together, the answer was no, not before 6 a.m..

On Christmas Day we always had breakfast, Rice Krispies. To this day I still don't like them.

The house was always trimmed beautifully for it was a truly magical time in our household. We used to race downstairs to find our presents which would all be in separate piles. I always liked mine on the armchair rather than on the sofa. Sean and Samantha's were usually on the sofa. We had to wait for Mum to have her morning cup of tea in her hand before we started to unwrap. Mum doesn't function without her two cups of tea in the morning. We had all the toys we could wish for and more; thinking back we had too many but I loved those early Christmases. We all played games together in the morning, even though waiting for boxes to be opened and batteries added always seemed to take forever. We used to spend a lot of Christmases at my Gran's house with all the family. We were all of similar ages so we all got the same toys. They were big family get-togethers. Then before we knew it, night had drawn in and we would be getting ready to head home.

Boxing Day we would visit my dad's parents' home. They lived further down our road and there would be more presents under their tree for us to open which we would play with throughout the day. My nan had musical carousel horses on her tree which danced and played a tune. It was very old-fashioned but beautiful; every year I looked forward to seeing those horses play. In the evening, more family would visit and we would play cards around the table with 2ps. I was never any good at the games but often used to win as aunts and uncles would help me out.

Dad wasn't always at home for Christmas as he worked offshore. Maybe this was why my parents split up and both Mum and Dad soon had new partners.

I was 10 and living with my dad as home life had got worse. I remember I was spending Christmas 2000 at my mum's. Me and my little sister were in bed. My 13 year old sister. came home completely drunk and smashed into the brick wall in the front garden before walking up the path at side of the house. Her nose was smashed up and blood covered most of her face. She threw up over both our beds before passing out. I felt frightened but we finally drifted off to sleep.

Christmas morning and there was a tension in the air which didn't shift throughout the Christmas holidays. Similar incidents became the pattern of Christmas year after year until I moved out and started to make my own traditions.

After my dad left and before I moved in with him, I would often get home and there would be a house full of people, lots of partying, and alcohol. There were lots of men and I never knew who any of them were. I didn't want to have a house full of parties. I never felt there was much love. We always had everything we wanted on our birthdays and at Christmas we were spoilt with designer clothes and things but ours was a dysfunctional family.

I moved in with my dad – then moved back to my mum's after a year. I can remember having my hair ripped out. It was the same thing happening over and over again. When my mum hit me, I don't think that affected me as much as her words.

A mum who didn't love me and a dad who didn't want me. I saw my friends with loving families and it made me feel worse. My dad had an 18 year old girlfriend. I did say some horrible things – it was a cry for love. I acted up to get some attention. We didn't speak for years; I didn't want anything to do with him.

My stepdad would flip out when he was drinking cider. I was thrown down the stairs. I stayed with my gran for the summer – but everyone was persuading me to go back and finish my GCSEs – then things got crazy – I was scared and my little sister helped me climb through the window to escape. I left and I have never looked back

The day my son was born completed me. It had taken me and my husband two and a half years to conceive. We found out I was pregnant just before we were going for IVF. Now we have the most beautiful boy.

My mum and stepdad make a fantastic nanny and grandad now. They are lovely people when they are not drinking. Things are a lot better now.

The Musicians of Bremen Syndrome

M.C. Gardner

Yesterday I walked to the stables. A bronze sky was melting over the walnut trees. I went to the stables with a heavy heart. Sunny had just finished his feed and the groom was brushing his chestnut mane when I got there.

'Sir, he knows you are selling him!' the young lad said.

'I know, but there is nothing I can do now.'

'Sir, I know it's not my business, but can't you just keep him? He's no trouble at all and he understands.'

'I must sell him. He is too slow. I can't afford to keep him. I need the money. I'm getting married soon.'

I looked at Sunny. The light fluctuated on his back. His hooves stamped patterns in the straw. His head was sunk into his chest. I stroked his head and his mane. I was sure I could detect tears in his… as if he knew… Sharp thorns pierced my heart.

I walked back to the farm and I had to pour myself a stiff drink.

A Crowded Shelf

Lyn Mckinney

Oh, that one's my favourite of Bert,
Next to him, our youngest child, Eve.
Something to do with her heart –
They did all they could, but
She went before him.

Tommy now, he was a lad,
Big and strong, and much taller than me,
He went off to learn farming,
And never came home
To Norfolk.

He lives up in Yorkshire now,
Selling animal feed in the Dales,
He's married with sons of his own.
I don't like to push,
He's so busy.

Bert and me on our wedding day,
'Course no frills, it was war time.
He was my soldier boy, and
I was his sunshine girl.
Tommy was on the way.

My friend Dot on an outing to Cromer.
Such a wind! It blew up our skirts.
We had ice cream and I broke a heel.
Me and her were really close,
But she's gone now.

Here's one of my brother Reg,
Came to me when wife Ivy died,
But he was already quite poorly.
We buried him near Bert,
For the company.

That's my niece June, lovely girl,
Came over a few months ago.
Said I should get a computer,
To stay in touch – I said June,
In touch with who?

She said, with the world Aunty May,
I said June, that's a wonderful thing,
But I talk to my pictures each morning,
And what's more,
They don't go away.

Night Life

Studying The Sky

Katrina Stockdale

Sometimes in the long light evenings of summer I go upto the allotments with my son to settle down his chickens. We take our dog with us and afterwards we take him for his last walk of the night. The Tumbler Hill Allotments are on the outskirts of Swaffham and from there you can see the night sky free of street lights.

It is so peaceful up there. You can dimly hear the traffic but the sounds of birds singing and rustling in the trees and hedgerows are fairly loud and, if you listen very carefully, you can make out each and every bird call. If it is a clear night we sometimes take an old telescope with us which my brother left behind when he and his wife moved to Blackpool last year.

We have two old loungers that we leave up there for me

to sit on as I can't do as much as I used to. I like to sit there on a clear night and study the sky. When I am leaning back, looking at the sky, I usually have one or more of the chickens jumping on my lap to see what I am doing. One of them is a Buff Orpington I named Ben. He's the biggest one of the lot and considers himself the 'big boss'. He is quite likely to knock my arm if I don't let him take a peek. He really tries to look but, as he puts his beak to the telescope, I don't think he sees much if anything.

Nocturnal Rock-a-Bye

Rhonda Peak

I used to live in Norwich. Before children – BC perhaps – night life consisted of theatre or drinks in pubs, usually with real ale and folk music. Sometimes we would see bands or join in at an open mic night. We spent a lot of time at the Waterfront, back when it was still smoky and, mercifully, you couldn't see what it was that stuck the soles of your shoes to the floor as the vibrations echoed up through your feet and legs and rattled around your bones. We would end the night with a sore throat, hoarse-voiced from singing, with an empty wallet and wrecked shoes.

After children nights became different. We moved to

Postwick and rented a house from a farmer. The nights consisted of the rustle of deer and snuffle of badgers on the lawn, punctuated by the hoots of a lone barn owl. Then, inevitably, the skitter of hooves and flap of wings as the wretched, needy cry of my own baby burst forth from an upstairs window and tore apart the peaceful gathering on the lawn.

Some nights after rocking, feeding, shushing, patting, changing, singing and desperate praying had spectacularly failed, we would drive around aimlessly with the now snoozing baby blissfully unaware on the back seat. To amuse ourselves or perhaps to convince ourselves we had somehow moved on, evolved, we would drive slowly down to the centre of Norwich and the Prince of Wales Road and score points for spotting local sights: two points for bare legs at 1am on a February morning; three for a girl with panda eyes crying in a phone box; five for an ill-advised kebab spilled across tarmac.

I remember one night on that very road, idle merriment disintegrated into anger and drunken brawling. We drove away, our tiny infant in the back rousing slightly and squirming as the car moved somewhat fitfully and the loud cries from outside took on a different tone from the usual raucous shouts of celebration. We pulled up outside Norwich prison with its enchanting facade of grandeur. An inky blue sky stretched over the peaceful city, at odds with what that building housed and the scene we had just left behind. My husband was already on the phone to the constabulary, telling his colleagues in that strange police language what we had witnessed: 'IC1 male, armed'. I twisted round in my seat to check on the baby; she was sleeping peacefully again. Behind us there was another car. It was clearly occupied. Josh, still talking, was pointing through my window. He raised his eyebrows. There were people huddled on the bench, staring straight back at me. In my sleep-deprived state, I had no comprehension of what was happening or why these people had gathered in the early hours of Saturday morning on a desolate hill next to a prison. Josh had a glint in his eye though and his report was coming to an end.

'Anyway,' he grinned into his mobile phone, 'you might need to send a car out to the prison. The doggers are out in force.'

He punched the button to end the call with a certain satisfaction and turned to me triumphantly. 'Ten points!' he declared, as he put the car into gear and we began our journey home.

Swaffham Discos

Camilla Balshaw

'There are no discos in Swaffham you know. Norwich has them not Swaffham.' Disco. It's old fashioned. It reminds me of Saturday Night Fever and the Bee Gees. It was a strange word to use; the estate agent was at least a decade younger than we were. Did we look like we were desperate to hit the bright lights of Swaffham in search of 'discos'? We only wanted to buy a house. We were not looking to recreate Studio 54.

As a 'yoga couple' our students have a pre-disposed image of how we met. In an Ashram, chanting, wearing orange robes. They imagine our first date. A decaf coffee, a small plate of chia seeds as we discuss earnestly the merits of headstands with or without a wall.

In reality we met in a 'disco', AKA a club, in Manchester at the height of Acid House. We're a product of nightlife. I have even been known to still appreciate a nightclub now and again but I didn't expect a burgeoning club scene in Swaffham nor would I like there to be a burgeoning club scene in Swaffham. It's not that kind of market town.

Then I heard the rumours. There was a place that

the young of Swaffham and beyond frequented; it even had a bouncer on the door. It had a late licence; it played music. Loud music. Before long I heard the first noises of those young people. Station Street. Midnight. The first sounds of nightlife would begin. The cries of 'I love you' slurred, unmeaning. The occasional fight. Click, click, stop. Click, click, click. Heels, very high heels, on sore, red, unsteady feet.

Now, I don't hear the howls or the clatter of heels. The place the young of Swaffham could go to to dance, drink and be merry is now shut. It stands on the corner. Grey. Unloved. Net curtains replace the bouncer. The older residents mutter good riddance as they put the bins out. The young make do with their phones. Who needs nightlife when you have Tinder?

Nursing in Norfolk

Julia Howarth

In 1982, I was living in Westacre, a beautiful and peaceful small village.

What a change from my previous life: living in a busy suburb of Manchester, district nursing in poor and troubled areas, with lots of high rise flats, broken lifts, smashed lighting and small groups of men smoking strange smelling cigarettes in the dark stairwells. And dogs too, usually thin and scruffy-looking. Often 17 flights of stairs to run up as fast as possible, carrying my large nursing bag, titbits for any problem dogs and fear in my heart.

Arriving and working in Norfolk was wonderful, and I fell in love immediately with the huge skies, the lonely lanes, the pretty villages and the people. I loved the job, my nursing duties were the same as in the city, but the country people were different. Most of them had lived in Norfolk all their lives and loved the land, the peace and the old traditions.

At that time, in 1982, there was no night nursing service and so the day staff had to cover any patient care needed. Thankfully emergency night calls didn't happen very often. The day team, however, was required to visit one patient regularly at night to give this patient an injection, and I soon had to take my turn.

I was new to the area and quite anxious about finding the house, even with directions. It was a dark night and there were no other cars on the roads. The house was beyond the village, down a long lane, no lights, no other houses, quite isolated with many trees and high bushes. And of course, we didn't have any mobile phones then so I couldn't call for help if I needed it.

I had my four young children and the dog in the car and I was getting more worried and feeling completely lost when my third child suddenly asked me to stop the car and look at the sky.

I did, and we all looked up.

'It's like Christmas,' she said. 'Just look at all those fairy lights.'

What a brilliant description from a seven year old. And so true. It was the most beautiful sky I had ever seen, so dark and vast but yet lit up with millions of twinkling stars.

Then we saw a light coming towards us and there was the husband with a lantern to lead us to his house and his wife. What a great relief.

'Come on, my woman,' he said. 'You've done well finding us. Many don't, and that's in the daylight.'

The visit went well. There was a roaring fire in the small cottage, and my patient was in the armchair waiting for me. The children were invited in along with the dog, but the invitation was gratefully declined. They were given biscuits though!!

I did that 9 p.m. visit lots of times and visited during the day too. I never again did see such a beautiful sky.

Sadly my lovely patient deteriorated and died peacefully at home, surrounded by her husband and family. She was well supported by our district nursing team.

I treasure this memory. Sadness, joy, worry, responsibility, the love of the family and their eventual acceptance of the death of a loved one. I was privileged to be part of their lives. I will never forget them and that breathtaking, beautiful Norfolk sky.

Gorleston, Swaffham & Watton

Gorleston Shopping List

Jane Rudd

1) The name Gorleston may derive from Gull Stones, a circle of ten stones which, some say, once stood in a field called Stone Close.

2) Was fishing port for herring and had own salt pans, used for production of salt which was used to preserve fish, until decline in Edwardian times. Then became seaside holiday resort.

3) Harbour at the mouth of the river Yare.

4) Sandy beach stretching south to Hopton.

5) Was historically in Suffolk.

6) Model boat pond.

7) Large council estates: Magdalen Estate and Shrublands Estate.

8) Sea air/east wind.

9) Easy to get from A to B as low level of traffic

compared to cities.

10) Limitations on what you can buy in clothing and food.

11) One fishmonger, when there used to be at least three.

12) Lighthouse.

13) Lifeboat station.

14) Two main hotels plus Travelodge.

15) It is rumoured that Charles Dickens stayed at the Feathers Inn in 1849.

16) James Paget Hospital built in 1981.

17) Pavilion Theatre summer shows and Christmas panto.

18) Golf club.

19) No cinema.

20) Library.

21) Train Station closed in 1970.

22) Saint Andrews Parish Church.

23) Summer Sundays at the bandstand.

24) Coastwatch station at the tip of the pier.

25) Gorleston F.C..

26) Ocean Rooms which used to be the Floral Hall, both used for dancing.

27) Appears to be disproportionate amount of over 50s.

Walking

Chanel Carlyon

I often walk around the town. I people-watch with my young son. It is a good place to go on a wander and visit the small, independent shops.

Gorleston is like a forgotten area, the roads are neglected, and the people are neglected. We require a lot of help. It's a beautiful place, Gorleston, but some attention to certain areas would improve the overall view. This is a nice, quiet area with stunning sites. The cul-de-sac where I live with my husband and son is lovely. We have a three bedroom house which we call home and we have great neighbours. We love it. Although there needs to be more for the youngsters.

What do I hope for? That this place doesn't end up being neglected further. A close friend of ours has set up a charity, the Anchorage Trust, to help local people here. I would love to get more involved and volunteer more. I will when I have finished my degree, working towards my dreams. It makes me feel quite good about myself knowing that I can help others. We hide so much emotion inside that sometimes having a person take the time to talk and help us can make a massive difference to our lives.

There needs to be more money spent on the place. It goes to the bigger places like Norwich and Great Yarmouth, doing up streets that have already had money spent on them but because it hasn't been done properly in the first place they have to do it all over again. If I had a choice I would spend money on lots of things, such as parking, pot holes, sign posts, small independent businesses. The area is so expensive for families; they just can't afford days out with the children as money is quite low here.

Walking is important to me. It's a time for me to think and clear my thoughts and focus on what's important to me: my whole world who I call my son. It's nice to be able to walk by the sea and show him everything. I also take walks with my friends, their children and we have picnics, use our trikes and play on the swings. When the summer season starts the tourists come down to visit and there's a buzz all around. You can feel the happiness in the air.

Seaside

Jurgita Stipiniene

I let myself join to the wind
And my mouth is open with the laugh…
How nice it is to be here
My hair goes mad, I am careless.

Gorleston Girls

Lyn Mckinney

A neat bungalow off the Beccles Road. The rain is threatening, but could hold off. I park in the drive, grab my garage carnations from the back seat, and head for the front door – but Sheila is already standing on the step. She's tanned, calm, and smiling, and in her late seventies. Hard to believe she lost her husband Harry a couple of months ago.

We sit down with a cuppa and there are four mouth-watering iced buns on a plate next to me. I give in and eat one.

'Yes, I lived on the Magdalen Estate… must be 50 years ago now…' course it was a different place in those days. We were all young with children, kids walked together to school and were much better behaved.'

I know what she means, though I suspect every generation says the same thing. I ask her if it was a friendly place to live.

'Oh yes, we were always having cups of tea together, and we would gather round the cigarette machine outside the shops – they wouldn't have that now would they?'

'Do you ever go back?'

'I see an old schoolfriend from those days – she's 81 now – and says it's not the same. Young children have got babies now; it's out of hand isn't it?'

Sheila was born in the Rows in Great Yarmouth – her parents lived in Cobham. Harry's mum took in Scottish girls who gutted the fish brought in by the local fleet. Sheila's grandad drove taxis for the Americans.

She remembers there were two picture houses in Gorleston, 'but Boots and Iceland replaced one of them.' I sense she's sad that the town has changed to keep pace with modern living. 'It was a nice, quiet place then.'

Sheila tells me I'm sitting in Harry's corner where his recliner used to be. Her eyes often wander to the shelf where there's a photo of them on their wedding day… he looks a handsome lad in his sharp suit, and Sheila, his bride in white, so radiant, both young and full of optimism as they cut their tiered wedding cake.

'Life was simpler when Harry and I were first married… I would get the bus to Great Yarmouth and it stopped right outside the house. He worked for a haulage company, and was often away for two or three days at a time. There was always lots to talk about when he got back.'

For a moment she looks like she might cry.

I tell Sheila about my friend Marion, who lived in Bells Road as a child. Marion thinks Gorleston is genteel, compared to its brash cousin Yarmouth up the road. Marion's father delivered the milk to the estate and her mother took in paying guests to make extra cash. Holidaymakers would often buy their own food and bring it home for Marion's mother to cook for their tea. And Marion had a friend who was made to sleep in the shed in the summer, so they could rent his bedroom out. Sheila nods when she hears that.

When I mention Marion's love, as a child, for the outdoor pool next to the Ocean Room, Sheila laughs. It had a proper deep end and diving boards, but has long since been replaced by gardens and a bandstand.

'I took the kids to that pool quite a bit. My daughter would buy a ticket, then throw it over the wall to my son, so he got in for nothing!'

Sheila was born, raised, married and brought up children all within a 10 mile radius. She still sees school friends and neighbours from way back. Whatever she thinks of the modern Gorleston, she has no plans to leave it just yet.

Marion moved away from Bells Road but visits regularly, and says people are very protective of Gorleston – and it's not just the free parking. Sheila likes that.

A Letter to Swaffham

Leah Spencer

Dear Swaffham,

This is the end of the line. I have had it with you. It's over!

You may have been expecting it; you must know that you've let yourself go. When we first met you always took pride in your appearance - clean, tidy, fun to be with, hard working – and you took good care of me. Now look at you – bigger, noisier, dirtier – you are flaking away. I know you try from time to time, on high days and holidays, but it's not working. I am bored. I need more.

Recently I've been flirting with others – Fakenham, Dereham, Watton – but I confess they all seem to end up like you, overrated has-beens. I need more excitement in my life and I know somebody who can give it to me. He's called Norwich. You might have heard of him.

See you when I'm passing through!

Yours optimistically,

Leah x

From Lithuania to Swaffham

Jurgita Stipiniene

A Fortune Teller

Many people ask me what brought me to the UK. My answer is very simple and truthful – I always wanted to learn more about different cultures, learn a new language and meet people from different backgrounds.

My mum gave me an unexpected present on my 15th birthday. It was a session with a fortune teller. Do you know of any teenager who wouldn't be excited about getting a sneaky glance at her future? At the same time I was very skeptical about what any adult, teacher or mystery fortune teller had to say.

The old (by my perception then), calm lady wearing funny clothes opened the door quietly and said, 'Follow me.' She showed me into a shady room. 'Relax,' she whispered. I felt butterflies jumping in my belly, as she left me alone for a while.

I looked around: the shadows from candles were dancing on the walls, handmade ornaments and various figurines seemed alive and mysterious. There was a massive oak table in the middle of the room covered in piles of cards and crystal stones. I sighed deeply and the thought crossed my mind – 'seriously, what I am doing here?' I suddenly felt afraid of the unknown. My thoughts were interrupted as the fortune teller came back and sat at the table across from me:

'What would you like to find out about? she asked.

I shrugged my shoulders and looked at her with a 'do-I-look-like-I-know' grin.

She just smiled at me and gently said, 'Let's have a look what we have here for you…'

The fortune teller slowly shuffled the cards and spread them on the table… One deck of cards had been changed to another and to another, my head was spinning… I can't remember everything she said but I do remember she said that I have a guardian angel looking after me and I will be quite lucky and happy in my life. She said I will have a few husbands and a couple of children and my parents will be proud of me… Anything else was like looking through fog.

I remember laughing inside, thinking 'yeah yeah, I bet you say that to everyone.'

'Can I give you a piece of advice?' she asked.

I nodded. I was bored by then and wanted the show to finish.

'You should concentrate on learning the English language', she said. 'You are going to live in a foreign country and it will come in handy.'

I burst out laughing. 'You must be kidding. We live in the Soviet Union.' I thought I sounded very clever. 'We can't even dream to travel abroad! We are lucky if we can go and visit another republic within the Soviet

Union without being suspected of being a spy.'

The fortune teller just looked at me and said, with a smile on her face, 'I just read your cards to you my darling... Learn English.'

Two years passed and Lithuania became an independent country again.

London

Many years later I found myself on the London tube. The air there was filled with different perfumes, aftershaves, all kinds of take away food and human sweat aromas. The carriage was stuffed with people, living the city life and rushing to and from work, their studies or just visiting friends. And I was part of it. I was caught up in the city routine – one child to school, another to nursery, and myself trying to catch 9.30 a.m. train to work. Family life, work and occasionally some social events...

Trying to understand various accents in London and learning to speak English without translating from Lithuanian in my head was a huge challenge for me. To find a job with very little English was absolutely a matter of luck. I had started work in small chain company and promised myself – I will put my all efforts to learn a language as quick as I can. Believe me it wasn't as easy as I thought it'd be! But my inner push was strong enough. My basic communication skills expanded every day and that gave me an opportunity to speak with more people and experience all that London has to offer – the charming West End, the famous landmarks, the food from different countries.

For the first time in my life I had tasted fish & chips, roast dinner, an English fry-up, sushi, lamb, Indian curry, Mexican burritos, Turkish kebabs and Mediterranean dishes. I have to admit I experienced many of these first times again and again!

I was happy living my life here and running like a hamster on a wheel. Until one cold day in early December I was rushing back home after work and my eyes caught The Tower of Bridge lit up with Christmas lights and decorations. 'What an amazing view', I thought and it shocked me; I was passing the Tower of London every day and didn't have time to notice it!

'You have to calm down and look around more often,' the inner voice whispered to me…

Luckily for me I ended up working with very charismatic lady who had become not only my manager but also a good friend. We used to be drawn into conversations for hours, discussing religion, the history of England and searching for our destinies. I've been lucky enough to meet lots of friendly and wise people who one way or another have led me to understand myself better.

On my holiday in Lanzarote I made a friend who lived in Norfolk. Enchanted by my new friend's stories about the Norfolk countryside, I decided to visit the place. And I was amazed by endless fields, trees, narrow roads and bright nights with skies full of stars.

My visits became more frequent; I had found a place where I could recover from rushing, smoggy, busy city life.

After 3 years visiting Norfolk I noticed that my heart longed to go back there more and more often. I realized I wanted to move there but the fear of unknown was unbelievable – not for myself but for my kids. Can I change their lives, their schools?!? The fear held me back.

Until one day I woke up with a clear vision, a message from my heart: it's better to look back on life and say, 'I can't believe I did that,' than to look back and say, 'I wish I'd done that.' The next day I gave in my notice to quit my job and start a new life... again...

I still remember one of my colleagues commenting, 'You are very brave.' I didn't think I was brave; I thought I was just trying to follow my heart and take a step out of my comfort zone...

Swaffham

And here I am. It will be 5 years in November since I moved to Swaffham.

I can't quite believe I moved to the place I didn't know much about. It has been challenging. The countryside reminds me of Lithuania but my knowledge, at first, ended there.

The first year in Swaffham I just learned about the place. I have to admit there's a huge difference between London and Swaffham. After 9 years living in London I had close friends, my job and funny, cosmopolitan colleagues. In Norfolk I felt isolated. It seemed like everyone knew each other and was suspicious of everyone new. My Eastern European accent didn't help either.

I struggled.

After one year I really wanted to go back to London where everything was known. My kids and I sat down to talk about it. I told them that I was struggling to find a job, find new friends and my savings were diminishing. My children came up with different views of course, one after another they told me how good it is to live in Swaffham – fresh air, a small safe town and they had settled well in their new schools.

I had to agree with my children – it's a beautiful gorgeous place to live.

We went to visit Swaffham museum. It was so interesting to find out about Swaffham history but most exciting was a folktale about the Swaffham pedlar!

The story told about the poor Swaffham pedlar who lived in a small cottage in the shadow of a huge oak tree and worked so hard to make a living but was barely able to provide for his wife and children. One night he dreamed a dream where he saw the great London Bridge and knew he had received good tidings that would transform his life. The dream came back to him again and on the third night he could not dismiss it. He set off with his little dog and walked the very long journey. Exhausted and weary he wandered around London Bridge. Then a curious shopkeeper asked the pedlar what he was doing. The pedlar told him about his dream and the distance he had traveled. The shopkeeper started to laugh and said, 'You must be a fool to take a journey on such a silly errand'. Don't you know such dreams are common? I have dreamt a very similar dream that I was in Norfolk – and in Swaffham no less – a place unknown to me. I was in an orchard behind a pedlar's house where a great oak tree was. I felt that, if I were to dig behind the tree, I would find a great fortune in gold but I am not so foolish as to take on a long and wearisome journey for sake of a dream!' The pedlar said nothing in return but his heart was gladdened. He went back to Swaffham and dug beneath the shadow of the great oak tree and found a pot of gold coins! When he emptied the coins out, he saw an inscription in Latin but was unable to understand it. One day a monk stopped at the pedlar's door and the pedlar asked him if he could interpret the inscription. The monk read it to him: 'Under me doth lie another much richer than I.' The pedlar dug once more and he found an even greater treasure.

My children's wishes and the Pedlar's story inspired me and gave me strength. The children had put effort into the new place and the Pedlar had had the courage and determination to follow his dream!

That stuck in my head and I decided I would make

it work in a good way somehow. I will show this place a real commitment! I will start to dig for my own gold!

Very soon after I ended up in a community centre looking for English classes. And the ball started to roll. After few conversations with centre management I started to volunteer there twice a week while improving my English. I'll tell you – the people who worked there knew what they were doing. I ended up answering the office phone, taking messages while they disappeared from the office! I got over my another fear – speaking to people over the phone; I had to dig deep inside for my English language knowledge and confidence.

After 6 months I had a certificate in my hands proving that my English knowledge is good and I had a job offer too!

3 years have gone very quickly by as I work and train to help Swaffham residents, finding myself again and again going through everyday routine and learning from people around me.

I wouldn't say my journey has been easy. I've met some people who have tried to put me down just because I wasn't born in this country, some people have been rude to me, some people have lied to me… Fortunately I've met some people who have brought out the best in me. And no matter what others say I try to live my own life, try to get out of my comfort zone from time to time and I do protect and explore my dreams.

A Recipe for Watton

Jayne Winterbone

Ingredients:

1 market town
1 wat or hare
1 ton or barrel
1 ancient woodland
1 wicked uncle
2 orphaned children
10 fluid ounces of Loch Neaton water
A dash of German wine from Wheeze
An assortment of Polish, Portuguese, Lithuanian, Russian, Essex and Norfolk folk
1 library
Charity shops, cafés, convenience stores and take-aways to decorate (optional)

Method:

Preheat the market town to 17'C/70'F/Gas Mark. (Hang yew hard bor, we're in Norfolk, your chance of having mains gas is about as likely as getting that there broadband for your compooter or City winning the FA Cup.)

Put that there ol' long ears on the barrel and set to one side.

Now take that poor little mawther and her brother

and lead them into Wayland Wood, add a wicked uncle (co ter heck a roight ol' wrong-un he wus) and leave them lit'luns till they're all a starvin', while that ol' waarmin he make off with their inheritance.

Take the folk of assorted nationalities and give 'em a good ol' mix in that there market town. Add the water and a good slosh of wine. Give 'em a good ol' stir till they be proper combined. Pour them into the library where they can have a roight good mardle and they might be a larnin suffin. Sprinkle on the charity shops etc if they fancy some troshing and cor blast me bor yew'll have yerself a bootiful Watton.

Now mind how yew go!

The Market in the High Street

M.C. Gardner

a line of stalls on parade
from Wednesday morning
to Wednesday afternoon
by Royal Charter
procured by Oliver de Vaux

a line of stalls on parade
in front of the Clock Tower
built by Christopher Hey,

a fire warning bell
the locals call Ting-Tang

a line of stalls on parade
melons strawberries, dates
samphire collected on the shores
and sharp fresh water crayfish
waft full-price at dawn

a line of stalls on parade
with stamping feet,
expert market sellers
smiling, catch your eye
their true catch of the day

a line of stalls on parade
wasps dive over the produce
lined up in cardboard boxes
money changes hands
for blue bags full of produce

a line of stalls on parade
melons strawberries, dates
samphire and fresh water crayfish,
for good measure on scales
and counting in the head,

all waft half-price at dusk

Watton

Gill Ashton

As I walk down the high street, the roar of the fighter planes, high above me piercing my ears, twisting and playing, chasing each other, practising their moves. Memories of my final exams at Wymondham College, long ago, the windows open as it was so hot and the old Nissen huts like ovens slowly cooking both staff and pupils. Above the fighters' screams disturbing my concentration.

The planes speedy on their journey and, in the sudden stillness, I notice the birds chirping, swallows gliding, soaring high, with their long tapering tails chasing insects on the wing. I remember long hot summers, sitting in tall dried brown grass, imagining their journeys to foreign places.

Blue skies are separated by thin wispy mare's tails; the sun so bright it warms the skin. These were the kind of days that I loved as a child; I'd disappear spending hours exploring and wandering through rippling corn, watching as it moved like waves on the sea, bending wearily in the gentle breeze. Poppies like red beacons dotted in clumps breaking up the sea of golden yellow.

The marigolds, survivor of the flower pots, orange and yellow waving in the wind, smelling of mustard, echoes of my dad's greenhouse where they were planted to ward off the greenfly. I loved to pick them, sniffing them, then sneeze as the scent overcame my senses.

Vehicles motor down the street, weaving between the parked cars, to and fro. People hurry, about their various tasks, absorbed, no time to notice, talking in languages I do not know. I feel like a visitor or a tourist in a foreign town. I should be on holiday with my family far away from my daily grind, relaxed, care free, but my children are no longer at home. Left, searching for a life far from here.

A closed shop with white-washed windows, all unloved, old poster curled at the corners. Its closure a result of the financial turn down; its customers gone, no longer able to survive; its employees redundant, hard times, no money but hidden from view, behind shut doors, with nicely cleaned nets, hiding the poverty from society, until the children go hungry.

Charity shops fill the empty space left behind. The musty smell of unwanted items, unloved, needing a new home. The smell, it's just like Granny Sadd's front room, don't hit the cushions they are full of dust, curtains always closed, and windows shut tight. No change of air, no light, leaving it musty, dark, grimy with the feel of being unloved.

A Journey Through Norfolk

Rhonda Peak

The cockpit of the plane is cramped and I can smell cherry brandy on the pilot's breath. John is squeezed in between us, the long line of his leg pressed against mine. The late August sun has sunk low in the sky and a dusky pink bleeds across cerulean blue. Cracked earth and parched yellow grass line the tarmac and, as the plane bursts into life, the air around us is disturbed, sending the gently nodding poppies into paroxysms of shock. Craning my neck, I take one last look at the aircraft hangar behind us. It is just a barn with peeling paint and a door which hangs on precarious hinges. Beside it, a dusty hosepipe is curled untouched like a snake. The plane wheels jolt through a pothole. We lurch forwards and I tip slightly into John who laughs nervously and shoves me upright again. The pilot grins across at us and mouths a question over the loud throb of the engine. There are two spots of colour high on his cheeks below slightly unfocused eyes. I think he is asking if we're ready. John and I glance at each other. John shrugs with perfect nonchalance but I can see his hands, long brown fingers stained with the juice of strawberries, his knuckles white where he grips the knees of his frayed shorts. It is too late now. I look out of the window again, just in time to see the world drop away and the poppies and dry grass forced flat at the shock of our departure.

We had been sitting on a ridge beside a marquee. The garden party was for the local landowners and as John's dad was a land manager – or a farmer with administrative responsibilities as he explained it to me once – and also a tenant on that land, John's entire family had been invited. I was staying at John's house that weekend, during that long summer between school and college and had tagged along to the party out of curiosity. Stretched out beside a bed of agapanthus and astilbe, bees stumbling from one to the other, John and I watched the guests at the party interact. The men had loud voices and ruddy cheeks and their uniform was camel chinos and a pink shirt, top button undone of course; it was a party after all. Their wives wore expensive dresses and had powdered cheeks and immaculate manicures. I could hear their conversations drifting across the field to the corner where we sat, unwatched: Miriam was off skiing in Canada and Jonty was summering in the south of France before deciding between the London School of Economics or a nice little position in Oxford. I was wearing scuffed Doc Marten's and shredding blades of grass with a ragged thumbnail. The ghost of one swallow of cherry brandy still burned my tongue, the juice of strawberries served with scones failed to chase away the bitter bite of it.

The man who ambled over to us, tired of the marquee and searching for mischief seemed to know John and greeted him cheerily, affording me a knowing wink. He could not have been further from the truth but I smiled anyway. He misjudged the distance as he sat down and laughed at his own lack of sobriety. The cherry-red liquid in his glass sloshed over his wrist as he waved a dismissive hand at the marquee in the distance. 'Stuffy lot aren't they?' he barked in the same tenor that was echoed back to us over the field. He was determined to be one of us though and we let him. He was at least twice our age.

He told us ribald stories and, when he threw back his head to laugh, I could see his fillings. It was when his glass was empty that he suggested it. It seemed like a perfectly normal offer for a Norfolk landowner. It was not at all peculiar that he had a biplane three fields over. We were sixteen. Of course we wanted to go for a spin.

It is only when we are surging into the endless sky that it occurs to me. With all the foolhardiness of youth, I haven't told my parents where we are. If it all goes wrong, they will have no idea and, while Vera Duckworth is shuffling over the cobbles of Soapland, my parents' sixteen year old daughter is soaring over the flat plains of Norfolk with an inebriated pilot and, more terribly, pressed against an unsuitable boy from school. It is August 31st 1997 and, somehow, it is not the strangest thing that will happen on that night.

*

The number eleven bus to Watton is parked too far from the kerb. As she leaps across the gap, bag swinging, displaying all the confidence of being four and on her way to her first day of school, my breath catches in my throat. I am four days post giving birth, which is four days post-operative and my tiny infant son is wrapped securely against my chest. The hand I have reached out to guide her across the gap is not needed and, instead, I rest it against the small form of her brother and feel his quick breath and the rise and fall of his snuffling body. His big sister has already disappeared towards the back of the bus and I can see her perched on the back row, one leg bouncing excitedly, her feet not reaching the floor. The bus driver looks me up and down and I try to remember if I've brushed my hair. Certainly not that morning but perhaps the day before, I hope. I know I must be slightly red-faced and out of breath from hurrying to the bus stop after yet another feed five minutes before leaving; none of my clothes fitting right and the wild-eyed stare of a woman who has not slept for days. I am proud that I can remember the destination and the number of tickets. However, the driver shakes his head. I panic that I am on the wrong bus. My chances of getting a taxi at 8am on a sleepy

Swaffham morning are almost non-existent. The bus driver grins and gestures at my purse. 'Put it away,' he shrugs. It is such a kindness on such a morning that I burst into tears.

The occupants of the number eleven are a community. I joined them as an outsider. On that first day, I sat in the wrong seat. Of course nobody told me it was the wrong seat. It was Barbara's seat. Only, Barbara was running late because she had stopped at the cafe for a cup of tea. I saw her that first day, shuffling across the road with a polystyrene cup, complete with precariously perched lid and I was faintly cross at her lackadaisical attitude. The bus could not go without her because that cup of too strong, value tea was for the driver and he would climb down from his seat and onto the pavement to drink that tea while catching up on Barbara's operation and precisely what the woman from number ten said to Barbara's husband in Tesco last night. This happened every day. The conversations were different but the tea, the shared cigarette and complete disregard for time were constants. They didn't speak to me at first. Sam would nod. Everybody knew Sam. He wore a football shirt and an open expression of amusement. Chris eyed me with quite open curiosity. Chris would often sing to himself and was delighted if anybody joined in. It took nearly three weeks and me nearly skidding over on an early fall of snow for them to become friendly. It was

Sam who caught me and Barbara who took my now howling three week old to comfort him. The driver handed me his cup of tea with a wink and just like that, I was one of them.

I even had my own seat (towards the back, over the rear left wheel arch). Barbara would pluck my son from my arms and settle him effortlessly and Sam would listen to my eldest reading her new school book, her finger determinedly following those simple words across the page. The driver would divert the bus from its usual route just to pick up some raspberries from a stall at the side of the road and then he would share them with the rest of us. It never mattered if I was running late because of a lost shoe or forgotten homework because the bus wouldn't leave without me. I belonged. My children grew up on that bus. My eldest progressed from Biff, Chip and Kipper to curling up on the seat and reading soundlessly, her lips not even moving to shape the words. The smallest emerged from his cocoon on my chest and learned to wave and clap at his new friends and even one day to walk unsteadily onto the bus, grinning at his extraordinary feat before falling over in a heap. It didn't matter though. Barbara was there to scoop him up and make it all better.

In the end, I learned to drive. It was a necessity for a mother of two small children living in Norfolk whose husband worked long hours and, as much as it was an achievement, it was also a sadness because I had to leave behind those friends. I never once paid my fare although I made a pretence of trying to every morning. The number eleven bus was fuelled by community, not by cash. Populated by pensioners and a frazzled new mother, I am still unsure as to how it made enough money to keep running. I wonder the same thing every time I pass it in my own quiet vehicle and see the same faces, perhaps a little more lined, hair a little greyer but occupying the same seats and having the same familiar, comforting conversations.

*

Looking back at myriad journeys across Norfolk and yearning for the past, it is not the heady swoop of the biplane that I wish I could re-enact. That night was fuelled by the recklessness of youthful friendship. In the early hours of the next morning, unable to sleep in our makeshift camp beds and buoyed by the adventure of that evening, John flicked on his television. We stood side by side in our summer clothes, the air now chilly and the sun long set and silently read the headline across the screen. Days later, the same television would show two small boys following the coffin of their mother, the streets lined with grieving strangers who had gathered to say goodbye to the people's princess. As we were flown through the still air on a late August summer evening by a man who had drunk too much alcohol, another man drank too much before driving somebody's mother to her death in a lonely Parisian tunnel. I didn't fully grasp the magnitude of that loss for those two small boys until years later when I had my own children and I acutely appreciated the life I had created where risk was never greater than running slightly late or perhaps sitting in the wrong seat on the 8am bus. They were two very different journeys during wildly different times in my life and traversing the Norfolk landscape in myriad forms was never more remarkable than the host of characters who journeyed beside me.

On the Bus

M.C. Gardner

She pulled up her rainbow coloured skirts as she was running for her life. She could hear her pursuer make ground. She might just save herself. At least she hoped with her new high-performance boots.

The rain was digging into her powdered face.

She could hear her pursuer breathing heavily. Her skirt was sticking to her slender body, the result of many hours of Zumba and spinning.

'Are you avoiding me, Amy?' She heard her pursuer's voice as she was about to jump onto the bus.

'Oh, it's you Graham! I thought it was…' and her voice got drowned by the revving of the engine.

As she sat down, she liberated her auburn hair from a crimson hat she had hand-knitted in year 11. She recalled she got an 'A' for it. The bus drove off. Graham sat down beside her, a smirk on his thin lips.

She did not like him. He had pestered her since middle school. She knew he went on to be an apprentice to a butcher in the neighbouring village. They'd lost touch.

Through the noise of the engine, she could just hear him utter, 'Why, Amy? I have got you all to myself now!' And as he said that, she felt a sharp scratch.

Her plump lips parted like an insect about to take off. The hairs on her arms stood up to attention.

'What? What?' was all she could utter.

Long Ago

Blackberries

Jayne Winterbone

The late summer sun blazes red, painting the sky in a giant sweep of flame. Driving home from work I pull the car onto the verge and gaze out over the stubble field. A brown hare sits up and looks at me with her amber eyes, before sinking down to hide in her form. 'I can see your ears!' I call, and in response she lowers her long velvety headgear. Suddenly another hare appears and bounds away like a sprinter from the blocks. My hare quickly follows and they race across the field, kicking up clouds of dust like buffalo on distant American plains. Four young roe deer grazing on the edge of the forest stop momentarily to see what all the fuss is about. I think about how this scene has changed over the past fifty years. The stubble will only survive a few more days at most before being ploughed back in to make way for the next crop. Although stubble burning had a deplorable environmental impact, a small pyromaniacal part of me misses watching the wall of flames crackle and roar across the fields, consuming everything in its path, roaring like some ancient god.

I always had a great sense of belonging; I wasn't just born in Norfolk, it was part of me, in my blood, a section of my genetic code. I was an inquisitive child, constantly questioning. 'Yud talk the hind legs off a dickie,' I was often told, but the older generations liked nothing better than sharing their memories with me. On rain drizzled Sunday afternoons I'd sit in front of a crackling fire listening to Grandad tell tales of being a teamsman in charge of the heavy horses, of horse whisperers and their magical craft, of the legends and customs of the farming year, cultivating a deep connection to the land and those who worked it.

Norfolk has been my family's home for as far back as we can trace; even my surname finds its roots here. I descend from generation after generation of farm labourers peppered with the occasional blacksmith or shepherd, domestic servants and washerwomen, plus the rather grandly named 'rural post woman'. Times have changed, maybe slowly, but there are still traditions, dialect, ways of thinking and doing that linger on in this fine county, and I am determined to keep them alive and kicking in this time of homogenous globalisation.

Life in the early seventies in a Norfolk village was a strange mixture of cultures, tradition and modern living. Norfolk has always offered a second home to people from across the sea, from Viking settlers in their dragon-headed longboats to Flemish weavers, Dutch drainage engineers who turned the dark damp will o'the wisp Fens into fertile farmland, the brave Polish airmen who fought alongside 'our boys' during the war, even the Italian POWs who were held in a camp nearby, all were welcomed into the community. These 'incomers' left their mark on the landscape and the people who lived in it.

The year I was born Neil Armstrong took his one giant leap, Concorde her first test flight and the microchip was invented, but people in the countryside still observed the old ways. My Dad was dyslexic and didn't learn to read and write until, aged thirty, he enrolled in an adult education class. Before his literacy revelation, which he grasped wholeheartedly, he amused us by telling folk tales and Bible stories from memory, and he was always singing hymns, especially good rousing Wesleyan ones; but there was a more ancient belief that walked happily hand-in-hand with this faith in the Christian God. No one saw any conflict in this, it was just part of life in the countryside.

Dad believed in planting by the moon. Country folk had used this method long before Rudolf Steiner wrote a best-selling book about it, and Dad followed this principle all his life. Potatoes were planted on Good Friday so the Devil didn't blight them. Preparations for this precious crop started months beforehand when

Dad bounced home in an old blue Ford tractor on a darkening autumn evening, a trailer full of steaming 'muck' following behind. This magical acrid mixture of cow dung and straw was transported wheelbarrow after wheelbarrow to the top of the garden where it would spend the winter reposing next to the wood heap, before being double dug into the black soil in spring, full of wiggly red worms, ready to work its magic on the newly planted tubers.

We had apple trees in the garden, but Mum also went picking in a nearby orchard. In those days the main fruit pickers were gypsies. Granny always bought her clothes pegs from them and never did trust the new fangled springy ones to keep her 'drawers' firmly secured on the linen line. We also had a fruit cage bursting at the seams with juicy scarlet raspberries, shiny blackcurrants, jewel-like redcurrants and tart goosegogs which, to quote Grandad Charlie, would 'draw ya arse up t ya elbas'! Blackberrying was one of the highlights of the year and we stuffed them into our mouths with purple-stained fingers and poked out our grotesquely blackened tongues at each other. Not only were they delicious, but Granny said they stopped you getting a cold, so we scoffed them straight from the hedge at every opportunity, but not after Halloween, or 'All Hallows Eve' as Dad called it. Satan was a disgusting demon and liked to spit on blackberries on this date, so they somewhat lost their appeal to us after then.

Old Nick also liked to hang around on stiles at midnight for some reason, while ghosts preferred crossroads (not the television version with Benny and Miss Diane which Granny watched avidly on her ancient telly, mug of Ovaltine in her hand). Just outside the village where my grandparents lived is four-cross graves, a crossroads where allegedly a gypsy was buried and his spirit haunted the spot. For years when we drove past there on moonless nights, with the mist hanging in tattered ribbons above the ground, my sister Helen and I would quickly dive under the coarse wollen blanket in the back of the car in case he made an appearance.

On summer evenings we'd hang over the fence, hoping to catch a glimpse of Dad, a smile on his face, freewheeling down the hill on his battered bicycle. If he was early we would load up the hand-painted blue Ford Cortina and trundle off to Hunstanton. We would race to the beach with a collection of buckets, spades and car inner tubes for rubber rings. On our seaside adventures we collected seaweed to hang on the wall by the back step to predict the weather, which Mum clandestinely threw away while we were at school when it started to smell like rotten fish. We also collected stones with holes in which we strung up and hung outside to keep the witches away. Today my house is bedecked with these 'hag stones' and it's an unwritten rule that you can't leave a beach until you find one, even my grandson has collected his own string-full to hang up at home.

We had a strange relationship with witches, on the one hand you needed to protect your house against them, on the other it was accepted that on Dad's side of the family it was common to have the 'second sight'. His great granny had been the village midwife and layer out of the dead, in the days when both these life events took place at home. She was a 'wise woman' and would be consulted on illnesses and life predictions. Modern medicine worked hand-in-hand with folk cures and in our household still does. In the time before the National Health Service, when my Nan's best friend died aged seven from diabetes, only the rich could afford the services of a qualified doctor. As children in the 1970s we rubbed Mum's wedding ring on our eye if we had a stye to cure and she used the gold band as a pendulum, hanging on a length of thread, to hold over my cousin's pregnant bump to predict the baby's gender. If we got stung by a nettle we'd spit on a dock leaf and rub it on the rash; quite a lot of saliva was involved, probably more than necessary.

Granny's best friend was Mrs Brighty. If you had a wart her husband would charm it away by laying a piece of raw liver on the offending protuberance. The offal was then buried in the garden; as it rotted away, the wart vanished. Thankfully I never got a wart. The meadow behind Granny's house was strewn with sunny yellow dandelions but she warned us not to sniff them as they 'make you wet the bed'. I was quite scared of this innocent flower until Dad assured us their diuretic powers only took affect if you ate them and told us instead of how the fairies used them to tell the time. Dandelion clocks then became our most precious find and always remind me of my dad. When, many years later, I collected him from Addenbrooke's hospital following surgery for what turned out to be terminal brain cancer, he was captivated by the seemingly endless golden carpet of them stretching out along the verges as we drove away from Cambridge. I'm still looking for the elusive little folk who use them as timepieces.

Lavender is a great fly deterrent and a bag under your pillow helps you to sleep soundly. Grandad had the most enormous lavender bush in his garden. Buzzing stripy bees crowded around it. We were never frightened of them as Nan told us how they pollinated plants and how clever and wise they were. Bees were sensitive creatures and liked a bit of gossip, so bee keepers always told them of any important events in the family such as births, deaths and marriages, so we would sit on the garden path in the summer holiday sunshine and have a 'mardle' with them. To me lavender is the smell and colour of summer. Grandad's friend worked at the lavender farm and harvested the heavily scented flowers with a miniature combine, his equally small dog sitting beside him. Both enjoyed a half of shandy in the club after a hard day's combining and sometimes as a special treat we were allowed to feed the scruffy little dog Walkers Crisps.

Harvest was the most important time of the year. Although horses had ceased to be used when Dad was a boy, many pre-tractor traditions lingered on. Horseshoes were given to brides as good luck charms and hung above doors to ward off the Devil. One of Dad's favourite tales was of how that busy old fellow once had a to do with Saint Dunstan, who pinched his nose with a set of blacksmiths tongs, and he's been none too keen on horseshoes, or blacksmiths, ever since. Grandad told us how on the last day of the harvest he took great pride in braiding the horses' glossy manes and tales with bright ribbons, the brasses, which kept the evil eye away, polished until they gleamed like gold in the sunlight. The field was cut from the outside to the centre, where the spirit of the corn would retreat to and hide. When this last golden sheaf was cut it was woven into a corn dolly, holding the spirit of the corn safely inside, until the following year when it was sown with the new seed and the spirit lived on.

I love harvest, the honey sweet smell of the ripened grain transports me back to my childhood. I remember loading up our bicycle baskets after school with cold tea in glass Robinson's squash bottles, Mum's homemade Norfolk shortcake wrapped lovingly in grease proof paper, and peddling off furiously to find Dad in the wheat field, following the billowing cloud of dust kicked up by the combines. As I reluctantly return to my car, the hares having disappeared into the sunset, I catch sight of the bramble tangled in the hedgerow, the ripening blackberries a deep burgundy. I chuckle to myself, the strutting cock pheasant on the opposite side of the road pausing to look down his beak at me, as I think of the squeals of delight soon to be heard as podgy toddler fingers cram glossy ripe blackberries into a purple stained mouth.

Nan's House

Larie Danson

I'm lying on my grandmother's high, iron bed running my fingers over the raised pattern on the white coverlet. My grandfather is sleeping lightly beside me, having his afternoon nap. I'm about three years old and I know that if I am quiet he will take me out when he wakes. I can hear his breathing and the birds singing in the garden. The room has a cool, spicy smell.

I study the chest of drawers in the alcove. It is tall, taller than me, and painted black. It has five drawers, three long ones and two smaller ones at the top. I can't reach all the knobs which are white and made of china, but I know they are cold, smooth and too fat to fit into my hands. The drawers are heavy. I can't open them which my grandmother says is just as well because there are private things in there. I've seen her take sheets and pillowcases out of the bottom two drawers so I think all the private things must be in the top drawers. They say the bottom drawer was my cot when I slept over here as a baby. But how can a drawer be a cot? Did they close the drawer when I was asleep? Was I one of the private things?

The chest of drawers stands on four wooden cushions called 'buns'. I can see fluff balls underneath and between the 'buns'. On top of the chest are three tall vases, pink with shepherds and shepherdesses painted on them but no sheep. The middle one has a tall lid. It rests on a black velvet stand with a glass dome over it. Propped against it, under the glass, are some broken wax flowers and a silver cardboard shoe. My grandmother says these are from her wedding cake. I wonder why anyone would put them on a cake; they don't look clean. I've been told they are from her marriage to the first grandad. I don't know him but I have seen his photograph. It stands in the back bedroom where I sleep sometimes when I beg to stay. His eyes stare into mine until I drop off.

I love being in Nan's house; it has lots of interesting things in it and she answers all my questions and I am not a nuisance. I'm sent to pick sage leaves and parsley when she cooks. Only tall grass grows in our garden at home.

A breeze flaps the curtain and my legs feel chilly. I pull the edge of the counterpane over them. The movement wakes my grandfather. He sits up, shivers and reaches for his jacket.

'Come on then, young 'un,' he says. 'I'll have a cup of tea and then we'll go out.'

This Morning

Charlie Dearden

The sun filtered weakly through the bedroom window. The duvet was more on his side than mine. Not unusual. I gulped down a glass of water and grabbed the mobile before the alarm went off.

Getting out of bed I heard the postman whistling as he closed the garden gate. Basil was pattering about, whining and getting excited as my brother Nick prepared to take him for his morning walk.

I quickly dressed myself. There were several things I needed to do before I set off for Swaffham.

In the kitchen Marcus sat looking at the post.

'Anything interesting?'

'The tickets for Madam Butterfly and the water rates!'

I sliced the strawberries onto my wheat flakes and added a dollop of full fat yogurt. 'Everyone will have to look after themselves this morning. I've got lots to do.'

Marcus got the car vac out. 'I'm going to hoover the car, get rid of all that sand. Don't mess it up when you go to Swaffham.'

The door swung open and Basil bounded in heading straight for his water bowl. Nick followed, wobbling slightly on his walking stick. He flicked the switch on the kettle and made himself a cup of coffee.

I went out to the garden room and began to fold up the dry washing, placing it in the laundry basket, which was when I noticed the wooden trunk which had only just come out of the garage – still not unpacked, full of memories.

I'll just have a look and see what's in there. Several files reminding me of when I worked, a few packets of old photographs and some hand-made birthday cards. No, mustn't do this. I must get on.

I carried the laundry basket back into the kitchen. Nick was finishing his coffee and toast. 'If you want me to drop you off at the fishing lake be ready for 11.15,' I told him.

I took the basket upstairs and distributed clothes onto beds. I had washed and dried them but they were capable of putting them away themselves; they were grown men after all! I got out my black suitcase and started to pack. Underwear, socks, leggings, t-shirts, but what else? I consulted my iPad long-range weather forecast. Lancashire: sunshine and showers. Well there's a surprise! Typical for England in July! Another dress went in, jogging bottoms came out. There would definitely be 3 key events; Sunday lunch with Father's cousin Elsie, Wednesday lunch with cousin Lisa, daughter Lydia and third husband Monty, and dinner on Friday evening with my best mate from school Pat Brown and her friend Margaret. Margaret had been Nick's girlfriend once; she'd been fond of wearing a full-length velvet hooded cloak which had made her look like Snow White.

I checked my phone. Time was getting on. I needed to print off my writing and then go.

I drove Nick to the lake and helped him with his equipment to the fishing spot. 'Do you really need all this stuff?' I asked.

'I can go fly fishing further up the river. There's a place on the other side of the bypass.'

'You wouldn't be able to get over there.'

'I'm sure I remember a place. Could you check it for me?'

I returned to the car. I had time to check, but I was sure he was wrong. He'd only been back here for three weeks, having spent the last 30 years in Australia.

I turned onto the bypass and slowed down as I approached the bridge. Gosh, he was quite right: there's a small lay-by with a No Parking sign and a small path leading down to the river. Who'd have thunk it!

Portrait

Katrina Stockdale

Until I was 10 years old I slept in the same room as my younger brothers and sister. It was often very noisy with the five of us. Occasionally I would sleep at our grandparents' house just down the road from ours. There I had a room to myself. It was lovely and quiet. I had been allowed to help my grandparents choose the wallpaper for that room when they decorated it. It was a pale green with pink roses; the paint was a slightly brighter pink. They also gave me a new quilt to match.

On the wall, opposite my bed, were two large pictures with a slightly smaller one sitting between them. This was of our great uncle Frank, Nanny's older brother who was killed in the First World War. He was painted in his uniform; his cane was fixed to the wall above and his medals were kept in a box underneath the framed picture. The cane and his medals were returned to the family after his death and were passed down the generations. My great grandmother gave them to my grandmother and she always said they would come to me.

My other great uncle on a visit to my grandmother decided he would like to have the painting, then after he passed away it would come to me. Unfortunately, his widow, my great aunt, decided to sell it as it had been painted by a very well-known artist who had been a friend of Uncle Frank.

A Haunting Memory

Enid Clarke

I shall never forget a night from over 80 years ago. I was a small child. I remember I looked out of my window at a blazing inferno.

The Barton's house in Mill Lane was on fire and it was just across the meadow from where we lived, in a thatched cottage. We children had been woken from sleep because of the danger of sparks landing on the thatch and the need to evacuate the house quickly. I can recall, as I watched, a vivid picture of flames leaping sky high and the tall fir trees silhouetted against the flames.

Mr and Mrs Barton lived there with their four children, two boys and two girls; Raymond, the younger son, was the same age as me and we were in the same class at school, often walking home together. My father had gone to see what help he could offer and it seemed as if we sat huddled together, waiting for news, for hours. When my father eventually came home, I can still see his face, blackened with soot. He sat down, put his head in his hands and, for the first and only time in my life, I saw him cry.

We knew that something dreadful had happened and he told us that in spite of repeated attempts to reach Raymond he had died in the fire. The rest of the family had managed to get out. There was a second tragedy a few days later then Mrs Barton died of shock and burns.

When we returned to school on the Monday, everybody was in shock. Miss Saunders, the head teacher, announced that we were all to attend Raymond's funeral and we were asked to bring posies of flowers. I remember my mother making up little bunches of lilies of the valley, gathered from our own garden. It was a very emotional service and at the graveside, as the small coffin was lowered, the children filed past, dropping their flowers into the grave. To this day, I cannot bear the scent of lilies of the valley or grow them in my garden.

Mouse Hall

Jan Godfrey MBE

Mary stepped from the car into an extraordinary stillness. Before her was a bare stretch of green sward, neat as a garden lawn, and beyond it a curved stand of sturdy oak and beech trees. The July sun was warm on her back and there was not a breath of wind or a sound to disturb the moment.

As she stood taking in the scene, her mind re-created the home that once nestled in that space – the home of her grandparents and their brood of children; a home that she knew only from a single photograph and her father's description of a solidly built farmhouse with cattle sheds and farm-workers' cottages. She could picture the whitewashed walls, the sash windows below and the dormer windows above, the tall brick chimneys, the turret with the little spire and then the weather vane with the mouse that gave the farmhouse its name – Mouse Hall. In her imagination she could see the children in starched-white aprons and sturdy boots playing under the apple trees, setting the hens, ducks and geese running. She could see the picket fence marking the boundary.

The raucous call of a pheasant pierced the stillness and her dreams. She became aware of lambs bleating - some of the thousands of sheep roaming the area, leaving everywhere their acrid-sweet scent. Behind her the sandpipers were darting and diving in and out of their hidden nests. Rabbits were everywhere, fearlessly nibbling the grass. It was a superbly tranquil haven for all kinds of Brecks wildlife.

Mary had yearned to visit this isolated spot in the heart of this Brecks wilderness. Some months earlier she had joined a coach party on an official tour, but it had not passed through the village of Stanford. She had mentioned it to the tour director whom she knew and he offered to bring her by car on a day when the area was quiet and so now here she was, gazing at the site where Mouse Hall once stood.

For a hundred years and more Mouse Hall had been a part of a small Norfolk village community, one of four neighbouring communities owned by the Merton

Estate. Several thousand acres of sandy soil provided a meagre living for the farming communities. Life was simple in these villages; the land was worked by tenant farmers employing labourers who lived in tied cottages. They grew or raised most of their needs and what they could not grow they bought or bartered in Watton, the local market town.

Over the years Mary's father had told her something of the history of Mouse Hall and the family (her family) who lived there.

The tenant farmer in the late 1800s and early 1900s was her grandfather John who, with his wife Elizabeth, raised six children who all attended the village school at West Tofts until they were twelve and left with beautiful copper-plate handwriting, their times-tables firmly in place and a general picture of where Britain fitted into the map of Queen Victoria's Empire. The two girls were married in their teens, one to a bank-clerk in Thetford, the other to a land-owning farmer in Suffolk. With the teachings of their mother to support them they created their own homes and families. The boys were in no hurry to marry; the oldest moved to Northwold to work with an uncle who had no sons, leaving the three youngest - Sid, Harry and Clem -to enjoy their bachelor social life playing cricket, ringing the church bells and playing cribbage in the pub.

They continued to work the land, sharing responsibility after John and Elizabeth died of influenza. The sandy soil of the Brecks is not good for growing corn and root crops, so they made their living from raising sheep which thrived on the rough pasture, and rabbits, sending a thousand a week by steam train from Thetford to the London markets. When war was declared in 1914, they continued to work the land. Farming was a reserved occupation – it was their job to keep Britain fed. But in 1916 with so many men lost, the brothers were conscripted. Clem and Sid to Europe and Harry to the Veterinary Corps in Mesopotamia, leaving Mouse Hall to take care of itself.

The War changed them; they left as carefree young men who rubbed along well enough together but, on their return, they found it difficult to go back to their former life. Nothing was the same; no one was the same. In the mid 20's, Sid, Mary's favourite uncle, was offered the tenancy of a smallholding on the outskirts of Thompson where he lived a gentle hermit's life until he died in the early 60's.

Clem and Harry soldiered on grimly until Harry met Biddy, a hospital housekeeper from Hazelmere, on holiday at West Tofts. They married in the 30's and took the tenancy of a small farm on the outskirts of Carbrooke, where they produced two daughters, the younger one being Mary.

Mary learned much later in life how greatly her father missed Mouse Hall and the friendly villages of his youth – Stanford, West Tofts, Tottington and

Sturston. But there was no time for regrets; when Mary was just nine months old, World War Two broke out. Once again the young men of the four villages went to war. Too old for active service, Clem, who was single handedly working the Mouse Hall acres, was required to 'dig for victory' – the Government call to all farmers to produce as much food as they were able to feed a hungry army, and equally hungry citizens.

Then in 1942 this unremarkable rural community did something truly remarkable. The British army desperately needed to train new recruits and needed land to train them on. The patriotic Lord Walsingham offered his land and persuaded his tenants to agree, with the promise that they would be able to return when the war was over. With just two weeks' notice, they left the homes their families had occupied for generations to make way for the army to create a battle-training area. Recognising the Government's need, and without complaint, they found homes with family or friends and waited for the war to end. Along with the other tenant farmers, Clem had to leave Mouse Hall and moved in with his brother Harry at Whitehall Farm, Carbrooke, bringing the family furniture which was stored in a spare room and his precious Ford Motor car which lived in the barn, seldom seeing the light of day because of petrol rationing. For the whole of his time at Whitehall, he started the engine each week, checked the car over and lovingly cleaned and polished it.

Used to living on his own and of a naturally taciturn nature, Clem probably found life with several small children trying at times. They in turn, and especially little Mary, were terrified of his frowning expression and his deep and always grumbling voice.

There is no doubt that Clem was a great help on the farm in those difficult years when labour was short, but it must have been hard for Mary's mother with two men, her own two children and two evacuees from London to care for. She never really settled to rural life, missing the street lights, the bustling traffic, the handy shops of her former suburban home but she made the best of things and kept the peace between the children and, indeed, between the men.

As time passed Mary grew more confident and less afraid of her uncle and in turn, he became more tolerant. Loving the farm and especially the animals, she trotted behind the men as they fed and milked the cows, she turned the handle of the machine that chopped the turnips and helped spread the hay. No doubt she was often in the way and occasionally one of them would shout at her, when she would run and hide, often in the piggery with Blossom, the saddleback sow with whom she shared her troubles.

After six long years the war was finally over and Carbrooke celebrated! An enormous bonfire was planned together with a pooling of precious ration book allowances to ensure an event to lift the war-weary spirits, but Mary was just out of hospital having had her tonsils removed and was not well enough to walk to the village. At first the other children were angry with Mary for preventing them from going, but her mother said she would stay with her while the others walked the mile to the village and the bonfire. But it was Clem who saved the day for Mary. For the first time in three years he brought the car out of the barn and drove Mary and her mother to the celebrations, while the other children walked with her father. It was Mary's first ride in a car and she felt like a queen.

The war and the celebrations over, it was time for Clem and the other Battle Area villagers to think about returning to their homes. But the Government had changed its plans; there was a need to maintain well trained military personnel in the face of potential new threats. Those who had lived in tied cottages who had not found a permanent home were provided with speedily built new homes in other villages. Clem and the other tenant farmers were given compensation and after some searching Clem bought a small holding in Rockland, where like his brother Sid, he lived a solitary life until he too died in the 70's. There was considerable resentment against the Government and Lord Walsingham, who was mortified that such an important promise had been broken.

When Clem died, the sole survivor of his generation was Harry. The hard work and privations of two world wars had left him with tuberculosis. He retired, taking his family to a remote cottage in Stow Bedon and spent the next few years in and out of hospital. Biddy was worn out with the work and the worry of keeping their two daughters at Grammar School; she died aged 57 in 1959. But Harry fought off all his ailments, worked his garden to produce most of his needs and when this became too much for him, moved in with Mary and her husband and their extended family in Carbrooke for his remaining years, telling them stories of the old days at Mouse Hall, stirring in Mary an interest in her ancestry and in the lost villages. Harry finally died just six months before his 100th birthday.

Now, years later Mary stood on that dusty path in the hot July sun gazing at the empty space where Mouse Hall had once stood, and thought of all who had lived in those lost villages, and of her family in the farmhouse with the mouse weather vane. Then with a sigh she turned and looked into the sympathetic eyes of her driver. 'Time to go,' she said.

Dancing at the Goodes Hotel – a memory of Marjorie Adams from 1940

Hilary Hanbury

Every few seconds there's a rat–a-tat–tat. Ping, ping: the metal benches take another hammering from the bombers overhead as the bullets pound the Great Yarmouth seafront. Two young women fearlessly sprint along, dodging them as they do every Friday night. They wear sleek dresses of mid brown-and-beige cotton crepe and their best court shoes with the highest heels. Necks adorned with Mother's pearls, lips painted the brightest red and legs painted with gravy browning seams. They laugh to mask any sign of tension they feel as they head toward their goal, a night of dancing at the Goodes Hotel where the best bands perform. They run the gauntlet of the strafing bullets whenever Tommy Jay's band comes to town.

Jitterbug and Foxtrots call for partners and a handsome Tommy awaits each of them every week. Sometimes they meet with the same one and sometimes they discover that the soldier they danced carelessly with one Friday night has been killed or wounded in action and will never waltz again. It's the whole uncertainty of life and death that gives them that determination to keep attending week on week. After all, death could be a matter of minutes away, at any time, so why worry?

All they care about is dancing away the memories of the day. Days full of oilskins and piecework at Johnson's factory. They spend every hour, from seven in the morning until six at night, making garments for the brave seamen who are defending the country on their behalf. The stink of oilskin seeps into their fingers and arms as they haul the heavy fabric around to stitch another seam. The lavender cologne does not always mask the smell of heavy duty work but they are proud of what they do to help the war effort, and rub lanolin into their calloused fingers. No medals are given for the oilskin women.

Right now, it's 7 o'clock on Friday night and they are ready to enjoy the freedom that dancing gives them. No time to think about the bomb that felled the house three doors up while Marjorie and her sister Hilda cowered in their own bedroom, because they decided not to go down to the damp Anderson shelter in the back garden. No time to think about when Marjorie's supervisor at work made them fall about laughing when he told the story of his father pulling the chain in the toilet and the house collapsing around him at the same time as the effects of a stray bomb hit the roof of his home. No time to think of the five friends at work killed together as they walked home from a hard day in the factory. No time to worry about dodging bullets.

Goodes Hotel, a force for good in the lives of most twenty-something girls in those dark times when each day you woke was a blessing. It was the start of many romances and was where my mum Marjorie met Leonard my dad. Three weeks leave turned into a marriage and two children. That's how relationships happened in the early days of the war. It was a 'now or never' attitude that permeated the forties; to live for each day and not worry about tomorrow.

Bang Mutter Grumble

Gill Ashton

Bang, mutter, grumble. 'You're too soft on her, in my day I wouldn't have dreamed of speaking to my grandmother like that.' 'But things have changed.' 'In my day…'

At this point I turn off, I've heard it a 100 times before, they don't know how lucky they are, they have everything. I know she's right, and yes things have changed from when she was 18 years old, and my confident and self-assured daughter has more chances and opportunities than I did, and much more than Mum or her mother (Grandmother Mitcham), in fact the whole world has reinvented itself from the time of my mother's grandmother (Grandma Douglas), who at the age of 40 felt her life was over, so she took herself off to bed to die. As a small child of about 4 years, I remember this very old lady, sitting upright in her bed, which had been moved to the front room of her terrace house many years previous. Apparently she never went upstairs as she had taken fright of falling down the steep narrow steps. Her room was shrouded in half light as was the custom when someone was not well or dying and even though she was neither the curtains had to remain half open. Her unmarried daughter still living with her because she was expected to stay at home and look after her parents into their old age; it was her responsibility. Great Grandmother Douglas had seen much during her life: Queen Victoria's death, two world wars, gaining the vote, the invention of electricity, and much more. She also had had 5 children without any pain relief and had outlived her husband and much of her family, the matriarch of the clan. She could take anything in her stride, until her 100 birthday party. The whole family came and, as a small child, I remember the 3 cakes with a 100 candles on each, the heat and movement of the flames were mesmerising. Poor Great Grandmother Douglas had meet her match; the look of fear in her face as these cakes were lit still remains with me many years later. Soon after she finally joined her husband and the mantle of matriarchy was passed onto the next generation.

Grandmother Mitcham was the youngest of the children, so was the baby of the family who was always made a fuss of by her older siblings. When Great Grandmother Douglas died the mantle was passed onto the sisters, each became the matriarch of their own families. As a child Grandmother Mitcham taught me and my cousins how to play cards and loved buying us Walnut Whips just so she could have one. As a young lady she had been to art college, a big deal then as many had no or little education, but once she was married she was expected to put her paints away as there was no place in her life for such things (Mother never saw her draw or paint). Children came fast. She first became pregnant during her honeymoon and then her husband was whisked off to war. The boy was born early and died, and Grandmother Mitcham had to deal with it all by herself; the only advice she had was to have another quickly. It was as though the loss was not important, only the achievement of living children was noted. Every time Grandfather Mitcham came home on leave, she fell and another child would be born. During the war her role changed, not just a homemaker or mother but also as a worker to keep the country running; child-care was undertaken by parents or neighbours. This all ended when the men came home from war and the women had to give up their jobs and go back to domestic bliss, with no or little chance of handling their own affairs, or so the men thought. Grandmother Mitcham never lost her new-found confidence and while she was not allowed to work she ruled the house and the family. She kept the family and her husband in check until she died, then the mantle of matriarchy was passed onto her daughters.

Mother's still troshing on about how it was in her day. How she met my father at 15, and how marriage was her only life choice and her greatest fear was about being 'left on the shelf'. Her parents' expectation was for her to get married, have children, and be a good wife. It seemed that there was no point in educating her; she wasn't expected to have a career ('it's not for women like you'). Her younger brother, though, was given the best education so he could have a good career. All Mother really wanted was to be a hairdresser but her mother didn't think that a suitable employment for a daughter of hers; suitable employment was an office job, that would occupy her time between school and marriagehood. Later Mother wanted to retrain as a nurse but again this ambition was dismissed but not by her parents this time but by her husband. Things had moved on from her mother's time - women's rights and freedoms, the introduction of the birth control pill – but it was still a man's world and women had to play the game according to their rules. Mother remembers being told by a doctor she would never have children if she carried on working, so she gave up her job for the family; a woman who didn't want children, who preferred to have a career was considered strange.

Mother now finds it hard to understand that my daughter doesn't have a boyfriend and doesn't need to ask permission to do most things.

This makes me think about how things had changed from when I was 16. My father's career advice was to find a nice rich young farmer and get married. I had to fight to be allowed to go onto 6th form, as he believed it was a total waste of time and 'as for' art college, well I was told I needed to get a proper job. To them a proper job was in an office, following in Mother's footsteps. I hate dealing with paperwork; I would much rather be creating, but that was what was expected so that's what I did. I knew it was no use fighting them, as father had already stopped paying towards my keep and I needed to survive. I was told again that I needed to find myself a nice young man. I did find a husband. On return from my honeymoon, my manager said, 'You'll be leaving soon to have babies then.' I was just 20. After that I was never put forward for training or promotion as I was a woman of child-bearing age and it was seen as a waste of money. Unlike previous generations I had one advantage, I could choose when and if I had children, and I chose to have just two children but not until my late 20s. The world had started to change, but not quickly enough. When I returned after maternity leave, I had a meeting with my female manager. I asked if I could work part time or job share, but this was greeted with horror. I explained that I wanted to spend time with my child while he was young. She couldn't understand this. I then asked about a crèche. 'No we don't provide this as you'd be spending every two minutes down there.' I left and sold cleaning products from door-to-door just to make a little money.

Things have changed. The employer who would not entertain job-shares or women working part-time now encourages it with child-care facilities provided. Businesses have realised that women can have careers and are just as good as their male counterparts. The law has also caught up as employers can't ask or assume woman are going to have children, and what my manager said to me would now be totally unacceptable. Young woman are not pressured to have children by the age of 25; many don't start to think about babies until their early 30s now. Also it's ok to live together and not be told 'you're living in sin'; I had to lie during the wedding meeting and tell the vicar that I still lived at home although I had set up home with my boyfriend. Women have access to education and careers that would have been out of reach even for my generation. But have things gone too far? A career is no longer an option; it's now expected. Children are left from an early age in child-care. Women who chose to stay at home with their children are seen as not contributing to the greater society. Looking after children is no longer given any value.

Have we lost something in this drive to being equal? Surely home is not just for sleeping in, it is where the family heart needs to be? I see my own daughter – confident, single minded, about to go to university, her life already planned out – with no time or need for a partner or family. She has more opportunities and choices than any previous generation, and her expectations of what she should do with her life are very different from mine. In time the mantle will be passed onto her, but will she want it or have anyone to bequeath it to?

Replacing Lost Energy

Leah Spencer

Show me a bottle of Lucozade and I am back in the front bedroom. It is 1954 and, though it is daytime and summer, the curtains are closed. The air is thick and troubled.

The double bed almost fills this room – an iron frame, a lattice of creaking wires and springs, wooden boards at our heads and feet. We lie under cotton sheets, woollen blankets, a candlewick bedspread. Under our heads lumpy pillows and a bolster. Sometimes the feathers pierce the coarse ticking and the soft embroidered covers, and prick us as we toss and turn. There are three of us in bed: Norah, Tessa and me. Same bed, same bedtime, same high temperature, same rash.

In the dark, I often parcel out this bed; draw imaginary lines down the sheets. Crossing these invisible boundaries can bring fearsome consequences. But now we are too ill and weak to fight. There is a truce between us as we lie together listening to friends playing hopscotch and marbles in the street outside. Their laughter and arguments drift in and out of our troubled sleep and fretful waking.

The stairs creak and Mum is here, imploring us to eat. But our throats are thick and sore, our appetites gone. She coaxes and cajoles but we cannot be tempted; we are resolute and tight-lipped. She searches under cushions, prises open the dark recesses of pockets and bags until she finds enough money to buy one bottle of Lucozade, which the advertisements promise her will restore our health.

We sip the syrupy sweetness from a tiny glass and its fizzy magic spreads through us. Reverently Mum places the precious bottle on the top of a cupboard, so we cannot reach it, and we lie there gazing at it, longing for the next dose.

Country Life

A Field

Camilla Balshaw

A field of dreams? Perhaps. I love the expanse of space, the quiet reflective silence, the sense of possibility, the feeling of being totally with nature in its full embrace. It's at these times I feel as though I've found my place, my home. I imagine a little cottage, brick and flint, a wood burner Aga (of course), the smell of home-baked bread wafting from the kitchen, an original stone floor. Floorboards shine and creak; the fire blazes. The cottage sits amongst the fields. Field and cottage: like two familiar lovers, a perfect union, content, comfortable.

Then the twitches of doubt creep in. I crave noise, action, people, and movement to replace those fields. I miss the anonymity of a city. I miss a good old concrete building. Oh, I'm full of field contradiction. Perhaps, I just want both? A field, with a nice artisan coffee shop nearby. Plus a good cinema, bookshop, deli, gastro pub…

Good Morning Stan

Nichola Lovell

Pink and orange radiate across a powder blue sky and the land glistens under a blanket of dew. Stan's Walk is a mile-long footpath that winds through the retired Watton Airbase. I stroll between its floral banks as butterflies dance with bees. Golden fields flank both sides of the verge and waver in the wind. Crows caw overhead as they fly, in unison, towards a copse of evergreens.

I sit on the white stone bench at the edge of the walkway. Tall birch trees whisper behind me. Beside me, statues of a pre-war farmer, a World War II pilot, and the legendary Babes in the Wood look towards the old runway. It is covered with animal pens now. From a distance, they look like vintage army tents, in a tight row, extending the length of the flight line. Am I a witness to the future covering the past or the past reclaiming what has been lost?

A flutter above me forces my attention back to the present. Two doves, in a feud, disrupt the peace in the trees. A troop of black birds cry out as they decamp in a flurry, and take to the sky. I gaze across a field of barley and spy a row of houses built upon the space an aircraft hangar once occupied.

Further on, twin cylindrical towers, like funnels on a steam boat, peek above the tree line. Could Reggie Kray and Jeffrey Archer see this beautiful vista from their cells? The meadows would have been free of crops and fencing when they were detained on the Wayland Prison ship.

I walked the old runway once, when I knew the RAF was no longer in residence and the gliding club had vacated. I snuck in over the ragged boulders that blocked the entrance. The airfield was camouflaged in thick snow, and my steps squeaked as I left a trail of my rebellion. The whole territory was mine for three hours. I smile at the memory and feel glad that I had the guts to invade the old base, before the barriers went up and the land was taken for crops.

I reach my favorite place on Stan's Walk where the path divides a grove of towering trees. It's a dark zone where giant stinging nettles defend the perimeter and I keep my feet firm on the path. When a gail blows, I like to come here and listen to the sound of the leaves like a raging waterfall. I marvel at how others – the lady walking her dog, the man on the bicycle, and the couple holding hands – can resist nature's primordial voice.

From here, I can continue on into the village of

Griston, past the 14th century tower of St Peter & St Paul's Church and The Wagon and Horses pub, built in the 18th century. But I turn around today, with the sun's warmth on my face, and make my way home. The wind kicks up a mix of sweet perfume and musty wheat, as I watch the crows touchdown on a strip of runway, yet to be concealed.

The D word

Camilla Balshaw

I am a woman. I am married. I am black.

I can stand on my head.

I live in Swaffham, Norfolk.

I am a fan of the D word: Diversity.

I am quite a fan of the M word too: Multiculturalism.

Repeat. I live in Swaffham.

So, why am I here?

I had barely noticed it at first. Driving through without consciously seeing. Swaffham was merely a route to the coast, where sea and sand sit together cradled by pine trees. I focused on the road, acknowledging at times the architecture. As I drove I pondered why so many Norfolk towns and villages end in 'ham'.

Norfolk's population is estimated to be 96% white British.

I am black-British. Born in Bedfordshire, in the town with an airport and an accompanying song to celebrate the fact. It's a diverse town. Pakistanis, Indian, Chinese, Caribbean, Africans, Irish, white British, Asian British, black British all muddle along together. There's a fierce loyalty to being from Luton. There is a realness, there's a take me or leave me attitude. It's never going to win any beauty contests. It swims against the tide. Consistently voted one of the worst places to live in the UK, it eyes with envy the more desirable postcodes that surround it. Its car industry long silenced, replaced by the hum of planes that fly resplendent over the town and beyond. Planes identified by a swathe of orange on their wings.

Why am I here? Why did I choose this particular place to live? Why does anyone choose a particular place to live?

I've always been driven by a sense of adventure, to experience a different rhythm to life. That's certainly why I spent five years living in Tokyo, a city not too keen on the D or M word either. To be non-Japanese meant stares. Stares of intrigue, stares of excitement and stares of curiosity. To be close, to actually converse with a black person, a real life walking, talking, black person. I walked loud and proud amongst the din of the city traffic. The snow-capped peaks of Mount Fuji overlooking the city like a matriarch. The Shinto temples cheek by jowl amongst the endless high rises. I could do no wrong. Why? I was different. Japanese culture is intrigued by difference, any difference, be that white skin, blonde hair, red hair, no hair. It was a seminal experience being a 'foreigner', a 'gaijin' which literally means 'outside person'. I was an outside person. You couldn't hide. You couldn't become invisible. I couldn't fade into the background. There was a sense of being constantly aware. I was aware of being non-Japanese.

I am aware too of being non-white in Swaffham. It's not essentially a negative. It's simply an awareness of being a person of colour in a predominately white area. You lose the cloak of invisibility. It's inevitable. You begin to notice other people of colour. The non-verbal and sometimes verbal acknowledgment of 'ah, another non-white person'.

People had commented on my impending move out of London. Not blatantly, there were no cries of 'don't move you're black'! It was nuanced; it lingered on the surface, the comments creating tiny ripples.

'I couldn't be the only brown in the village.'

'You're so brave.'

'You'll stand out.'

At a party in East London in 2016 making small talk.

Man: 'So, what do you do?'

Me: 'I'm a Iyengar yoga teacher. I have a studio in my home.'

Man: 'Where's home?'

Me: 'Norfolk, well. . . a little market town called Swaffham.'

Man: 'Norfolk.'

He says this slowly, deliberately, his eyes giving away his shock, his incredulity.

Man: 'Now, that's different.'

The conversation then took on a surreal turn. He thought I was playing some sort of joke on him. He started laughing. I let him. I declined to pass on the small detail of my name. It had history but more of that later.

Man: 'You're called Camilla. You teach yoga. You live in Norfolk and you live in a Georgian house.'

Here is the image we have. I'm guilty of this too. We all create a single story in our heads.

Urban = a melting pot.

Rural = a non melting pot.

He walked away. Laughing, shaking his head as though the more he shook it the more sense it would make. I looked around the room. I was in East London, the home of the D and M word and here I was 1 of 2 non-white faces in the room. An urban melting pot?

And so back to the small detail of my name, or what could be described as 'The Great Luton Name Clash'. Camilla or Amanda. The names fought by two opposing factions. My Nigerian father and my Jamaican mother. Two strong personalities they clashed spectacularly. Not only due to the chasms of being from the Caribbean and Africa (not a natural coupling). As a middle-class Nigerian my father wanted to call his last daughter something truly English, grand sounding, Camilla. My mother, from St Thomas, a hidden gem of Jamaica not far from Kingston, favoured a much more low-key sounding name, Amanda. These two opposing names, Camilla and Amanda chosen by a couple of the Commonwealth became a sticking point. It was the bleak winter of January 1970, my mother's 10th winter in England. She had been lured to English shores, as had many in the 50s and 60's, by the promise of work and to help build the new exciting 'motherland'. Jamaica had a firm loyalty to England right up until Jamaica gained independence in 1962. For my mother's generation the bond between the two nations was unbreakable, indestructible like the best steel. My father had come to England solely with the idea of becoming a Nigerian version of an English playboy. A deal was agreed. They settled on an uneasy truce. My birth certificate, full name Camilla Adebisi; however I was to be known as Amanda. Amanda was to be my 'pet' name. A pet name is a common occurrence in the Caribbean. It's a name given as a term of endearment. Many of my mother's Jamaican friends have a pet name. For years someone I thought of with affection as Gloria turned out to be called 'Sally'. In the spirit of the pet name I went along with it. I had no choice at the time. I was born as Camilla AKA 'Amanda' or 'Mandy'. I grew up knowing full well my 'real' name was Camilla; secretly I kind of liked it but growing up in Luton 'Mandy' was a perfect fit. It was un-showy, I didn't know any Camilla's, and I wanted to blend in. It wasn't until my early 20's that I began to have second thoughts. I did like the name Camilla. I even quite liked my very Nigerian sounding middle name. I wanted ownership. I wanted my full name back.

Growing up in the 80's an African-sounding middle name was not a good thing. Everyone associated Africa with poverty, mud huts, swollen bellies. The entrepreneurial, driven, ambitious side of the continent was rarely shown. I hid my African connection and proudly emphasised my Jamaican heritage. Jamaica was cool. They had reggae, cool ways of speaking; this was the 80's so they were good at cricket too. I didn't want Nigeria with its strange head wraps. I wanted to blend in. I became a hybrid of Luton and Jamaica although my mother hardly ever spoke patios at home. This was far too common and meant I could never get a good Jamaican patios accent. I sounded embarrassingly similar to Jim Davidson. I was hopeless at it.

Why am I here?

Perhaps the answer lies in part to my heritage. The great wave of Commonwealth immigration in the 50s and 60s came to England in the main from rural communities in the Caribbean, Africa and India. The immigrants felt no great affinity to or a connection with cities. They felt no kinship with urbanisation, its sprawl, its people, or the concrete that replaced nature.

They were instinctively drawn to the countryside. Although work, jobs and family dictated many had to gravitate to the city for survival. Is this why I am here in Swaffham? It's a legacy of my parents; their rural heritage kept alive by my retreat to Swaffham?

Or was it a building? I've lived in cities for most of my life, that's where I thought I belonged but a sad, bewildered building, unloved, uncared for has drawn me away. It stood slightly hidden behind overgrown climbers, which had congealed and resembled a large dreadlock. A crack ran through the outside chimney as though the house had had its heart ripped out. The house cried out to be saved and brought to life. To be reincarnated as a place to serve the community. It was a gamble, but slowly it's paid off. There is no doubt this is the main reason for living here. To see the house transformed as a place to make a difference to people's lives.

My relationship with Swaffham is more complex. It's similar to a pair of size 8 jeans. They sit on the hanger. You've passed them a few times. You think they might be unsuitable. You take a deep breath, you wriggle and fight, and somehow you manage to squeeze into them. Not a natural fit, but it works. To make it work I frequently have to take off those jeans and wear something more comfortable. For those moments when I need the D and M word, just a little more action, a little more stimulation, I go to the cut and thrust of a city.

Right now there is added spice and twist to living here. Two years ago my mother moved from Luton to Norfolk. She lives not too far from Swaffham. She tends her garden, she attends a local church and talks of the supportive community around her. She notices and acknowledges the other Carribeans, Africans and Asians she meets. First generation immigrants who came in 60s, they now call Norfolk home. She says she was witness to my own contentment living here. That's why she moved. On visits she and her husband would disappear. They had a favoured spot. They would sit on a bench and watch over the town like two sentinels. Two rural Jamaicans, quietly observing the ebb and flow of life in rural Norfolk.

My sister has also moved to… Norfolk. They have settled within the last year in a smaller, close-knit village not too far from Swaffham.

The D and M word have been upped incrementally by the arrival of my family. I like that. A small change but significant.

I'm constantly asked how long I'll stay living in Norfolk. I ask myself the question frequently too. For now it's home; for how long, well… who knows? At the moment those inappropriate jeans are fitting a little more comfortably.

District Nursing

Julia Howarth

Arriving in Norfolk and starting work as a district nurse almost immediately was amazing. The countryside beautiful but the villages spread out. Finding them was difficult for a stranger in 1981. No mobile phones or Sat Navs. Just blurry printed maps of places that I had never heard of. Not being a natural navigator it took quite a long time to find my way about. Sometimes I even had to drive as far down as the Suffolk border.

Most Norfolk people were wonderful, helpful and kind when I visited them, supplying me with fresh lettuce and parsley which they soon got to know I loved. It was all gratefully accepted and appreciated.

But I did make some mistakes and I will never forget being invited into a tiny bungalow to see an elderly male patient. The sitting room was full of smoke and the very thin and poorly looking man was puffing on a cigarette, as was his wife.

After a few moments of trying to speak without coughing and spluttering, watery-eyed I politely asked the man if he could please put his cigarette out whilst I took his details and renewed his dressing. He immediately lost his temper and told me in no uncertain terms that it was his f---ing house and he could f---ing well smoke where and when he wanted to. I was really shocked but what he said was true: district nurses are guests in people's houses and unless the situation is very dangerous it is policy to abide by their rules and lifestyle.

So I carried on and did what I had to do, apologised for upsetting him and I explained that it was his health I was thinking about and arranged for a prescription for pain killers and to visit again in two days. He said nothing but his wife was upset and came to the door with me. I remember telling her not to worry, that it didn't matter, and I'd heard much worse as a district nurse in Manchester and Salford, which was true.

So two days later I knocked at the door feeling rather apprehensive. What a difference! The living room had a faint smell of cigarettes but no evidence of recent smoking and the patient was up and out of the chair, shaking my hand and apologising for his behaviour.

In the months that followed we developed a good and beneficial relationship; his leg healed and he was able to get to Swaffham Market again, something that he had really missed. But he never did stop smoking, except when I visited.

There were many patients that I will never forget:

A beautiful young girl dying at home and lying in her coffin in the wedding dress that she never got to wear when alive.

A handsome and positive young man who had an amputation for melanoma of the leg. Sadly the cancer reoccurred and this patient died.

And Jane an elderly lady who shared her life with a pet hen who used to sit by the fire with her, getting an occasional stroke. Jane's little house was spotless and the wooden floorboards upstairs shone with lavender polish.

She was such a lovely old lady, a childless widow with very challenging health problems. She always baked scones on the day that I visited and, yes, I did succumb. A scone, a quick cup of tea, and a chat. An extra ten minutes that made a difference to both our lives.

What was extraordinary was that she told me a secret that I had to promise not to report to anyone in authority. As this was more than 35 years ago I feel that I can reveal what she told me. She had a regular visit from a local clerical member of one of the Norfolk churches. She enjoyed the visit, the company and, no doubt, he also went away with a scone or two. However he also went away with a bag of her coal which he took without her permission after every visit.

What a dilemma! I said that he should be reported or that I could have a word with him and ask him not to steal her coal. However Jane had strong and fixed ideas about this and said that he must have been very cold and she didn't mind. She was glad that she'd found out because she'd thought she'd been using her coal up rather quickly. I remember her saying, 'Poor man, his need must be much greater than mine.' She thought him a bit odd but he was always kind to her.

I kept her secret but did ask a local handyman to put a lock on her coalshed door. She agreed with this and we often had a laugh about the person concerned being thwarted and having to buy his own coal!!! He still visited but the visits grew slightly less frequent. Jane was happy with the situation.

She was well into her late eighties when she died and I will never forget her.

For years I was a District Nursing Sister working in the villages surrounding Swaffham and Downham Market and then I became the main carer of my husband David who has Parkinson's disease and Dementia and I have my own problems with heart disease. I have had wide experience of illness, both personal and professional, and the management of long-term health problems in this part of Norfolk.

Lasting friendships with both colleagues and patients have been fulfilling. The work was often full of inevitable sadness for the team, the patients and their relatives, but often too there was laughter as well as tears, and sometimes the most remarkable recoveries.

Egg-bound

Nichola Lovell

Whistling a tune as he closed the door behind him, he bent over and filled a sombrero-shaped water dish from a bucket. A hoard of chickens mulled around his feet, clambering over one another clucking and moaning. I called out to him, 'Morning Einstein!'

He straightened as I got near and flashed me a full-toothed smile. Lifting the front of his patchwork Ivy Cap, he scratched his forehead before settling it back over a fleece of silver-white hair. Stepping closer, he said, 'Well, good mornin' my beauty! How ya doin' on?'

I beamed at him through the chicken wire. 'I'm doing good thanks, old man, how are you?'

Amusement lit up his ice blue eyes, and he shook his head. 'I'm not bad, my beauty, not bad at all. Sun's a shinin', a cool breeze is a blowin'.' He leaned towards me, tipped his head and patted his stomach. 'I got a full belly, so I got no complaints.'

'Can I give you a hand?'

'Oh, well now, that's an offer in't it?' He glanced down at the chickens pecking his feet, and said, 'But no, no, I shall be done soon enough.' Then he lifted his head, his eyes focussed somewhere over my shoulder, nodded and pointed. 'You should go on up to the house and surprise Pearl, she'll like to see you.'

'I already have, I thought I'd come out here and enjoy the fresh air for a bit. You sure there's nothing I can do?'

He heaved in a breath then let it out in a loud puff. 'Ahhh… well.' He tucked his hands into the pockets of his worn slacks and rocked back on his wellied heels. 'I s'pose you can run up to the shed there, grab yourself a bucket and collect the eggs, if you want?' Thick white eyebrows disappeared under the brim of his cap.

Squaring my shoulders, I clicked my heels together and honoured him with a salute. 'Alrighty Cap'n.' I made my way to the shed.

Einstein was in the second enclosure, replenishing the water supply, by the time I came back. I approached the first cage and my presence caused an immediate uprising. The hens rushed against the door, pushing, pecking and warbling.

'Don't let the noisy buggers crowd you now, just step on in and they'll move outta your way. You won't hurt 'em, my gal!'

Raising my arm, I gave a thumbs up. On opening the door, just enough to get my foot in, a chicken jumped onto my sneaker. Its wings flapping stray plumage into the air. 'Hey lady! Knock it off!' Pushing my knee into the gap, I got my right leg in, did the hokey pokey and managed to shake her loose. Inch by inch I forced myself through the breach. Using the bucket as my shield, I pushed back the gibbering swarm until I could turn and close the door without escapees. 'Phew!'

I looked over to see Einstein leaning against the hen house next door, one elbow resting on the roof, and one boot clad foot crossed over the other. His shoulders shaking so much, if not for his snickering and a finger wiping at his eye, I'd swear the man was doing a shimmy.

My hands were on my hips before I knew it, the bucket resting askew next to my thigh. 'You laughing at me?' I could hardly get the words out for my own giggling. Watching Einstein crack-up, even if I was the butt of his joke, was a treat. He turned around, but I could still see his shoulders shaking under his body warmer.

I tried to be more assertive as I made my way through

the humming flock. Upon reaching the large yellow bird house, I grabbed the lid to the laying area and started to pull it up. The lid was halfway open when my eyes fell upon a chicken inside. The lid came slamming down as I jumped back in surprise! 'Oh Jeeeezuss!' My cry a breathless whisper. A few moments passed, as I stood clutching my chest and waiting for the drum beat in my ears to subside.

Peeking a glance over at Einstein, I was relieved to see he was oblivious. I lifted the lid again, and pushed it back onto its hinges. The hen remained snoozing. Not wanting to force her out, I gave her a gentle poke, her feathers silky soft against my finger. She opened her eyes and closed them again. No other movement or complaints came from her. I'm no expert with nesting hens, but I expected some form of protest.

Glimpsing movement to my left, I looked up to see Einstein traipsing past, smiling from ear to ear and swinging a bucket in each hand. I waved to get his attention.

'Everythin' alright, my beauty?'

'Uh, there's a hen in one of the boxes. She's not moving or saying much.'

'Oh she's probably just clucky.' He dropped his buckets and came inside. A few chickens flew up in front of him, but he marched headlong through the mob. 'You've just got to pick her up and toss her out, gal.' He was beside me in seconds and stuck a large rough hand into the nesting area and went to grab her, but his hand stopped short of picking her up. Bending his knees, he leaned his head all the way in and over her. 'Hmmmm.'

He ducked his head out, breathed a sigh and reached back in. Wrapping both hands gently around her sides, he lifted her with the carefulness of a bomb disposal expert. When she was halfway out, I could see that a mass of congealed blood and bits of eggshell were stuck to the feathers around her rear end.

I gasped. 'Oh God! What's wrong with her?'

With all humour gone from his face, he shook his head. 'Egg-bound with old age, I'm afraid.' He pulled her towards him and cradled her in his left arm.

'Oh, you'll have to call the vet out then, will you?'

Glancing from the hen to me, 'No, my beauty, no need for a vet.'

My face grew hot. 'Oh. Of course. You already know what to do. You've been caring for chickens, probably, since you were a young boy, right?'

'Well, yes yes, you are right, my gal, you are indeed right about that.'

'So, what do you do when this happens?'

He looked at the hen in the crook of his arm, ran his index finger down the feathers on her back, slid his hand around her neck and twisted. A sharp knuckle-crack pierced the air as her neck fell limp and dangled over his thick forearm.

My hand flew to my mouth as I cried out. I'd never

witnessed anyone kill anything bigger than a spider in my life!

I looked up at Einstein. His eyes apologetic and his voice light but firm, he said, 'That's what you do, my beauty. Quick and painless.' He turned, strode out of the cage, lobbed the hen's warm lifeless body onto the compost heap, picked up his buckets and continued on, whistling his tune.

The Cherry Red Door

Jayne Winterbone

The summer sun warms my back as I wander along the High Street. My gaze strays to the empty shop at the end of the street, its blind-eyed white smeared windows and peeling paint announcing its loneliness to the world. Next door the old brewery stands tall and proud in its gleaming new white coat and cherry red door. The rejuvenated exterior hides from eyes that don't bother to pry too deeply the 'serviced apartments', several migrant workers shoe-horned into each one, making rich the landlord in his new 4x4, the size of a small house; rural poverty concealed behind a plush exterior.

A truck packed with squealing pigs rattles past on

their final trip to the abattoir. Their piggy smell wafts past, their snouts squeezed through the bars. A pang of sadness and despair grips my guts. I try not to think of their doom as I turn away, feeling helpless.

Flatlands

Camilla Balshaw

He told me they come here to die.
The flatlands.
Where witches were burnt.
Where sky meets earth.
Where voices carry through the market.
He told me they come here to die.
They seek a quiet life.
A little England.
Safe.

Contributors

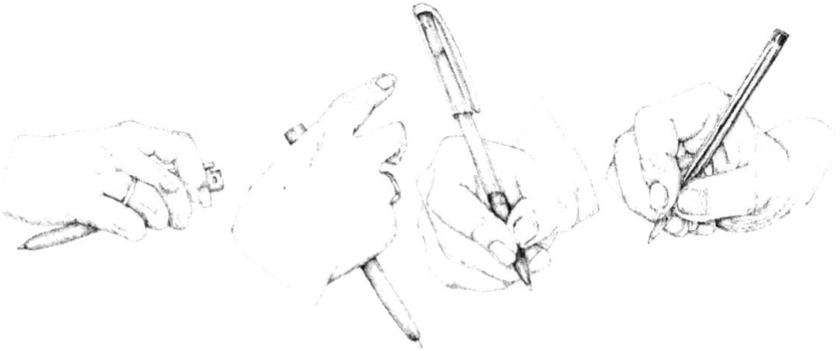

Gill Ashton is a long suffering dyslexic, who after many years of being scared to put words on paper realised that all those negative people who said she couldn't write were in fact wrong. Actually, dyslexia is not a limit but a blessing, especially with the introduction of spell check! Don't allow others to limit your dreams, as anything is possible if you put your mind to it.

Camilla Balshaw is an aspiring writer (with an awful lot to learn). She has lived in Norfolk for 6 years. She can do a pretty good downward facing dog pose and is always on the lookout for good coffee and cake.

Lynne Bryan is the author of a short story collection, Envy At The Cheese Handout (published by Faber & Faber), and the novels Gorgeous and Like Rabbits (Sceptre). Her work has been included in many anthologies and has been broadcast on the radio and adapted for film. She is co-organiser of Words And Women.

Chanel Carlyon: I am 25 years of age, married and a mum to one gorgeous little boy. I have spent most of my life growing up in Great Yarmouth and the Gorleston area and see how things have changed. I've suffered with dyslexia all my life before being diagnosed in May 2015, but I've not let my struggle stop me from achieving my dreams. I am currently working towards my foundation degree with the hope that one day I can become a teacher. I work in a nursery caring for children under 5 which I absolutely love. I feel strongly about helping others and hopefully one day I will be in a situation to help on a more permanent basis, volunteering and helping friends with their charity, which they have set up designed to help local people with recruitment and housing. I strongly believe good deeds are rewarded, so my mission now and for the future, is to donate tins and toiletries to our local food bank, as we never know what's around the corner. One day that could be any of us needing help. Live every day to its fullest. Love, laugh and be happy.

Enid Clarke is in her nineties and apart from three years working away during the Second World War has lived all her life in Carbrooke. After bringing up her two sons she then found time to further her interest in art which she did with some success. With her husband, Jack, she enjoyed visiting her sister in America and another sister in Scotland. She loves writing and occasionally has articles published in the local village magazine. She adores her great grandchildren and loves spending time with them.

Rose Cowan is an illustration graduate from Norwich University of the Arts. While at university Rose's final piece was long-listed for the Ruskin Drawing Price. She was also selected by her tutors to curate the BA final show and the graduate stall for D&AD New Bloods. Rose has designed book covers for Hodder & Stoughton and Words and Women. She will be attending the Royal Drawing School in London this autumn.

Larie Danson: ex-wife, ex-teacher, now lives in Swaffham with an ageing, red-haired athelete.

Charlie Dearden has spent most of her life involved in the arts. She started her working life as a teacher but encouraged by friends, involved in community arts projects, she was persuaded to build and burn a Viking Boat in the sea at Hunstanton. This led to a career change and a move away from Norfolk. She called herself a creative producer and enabler, assisting, supporting and creating opportunities for artists to reach their full potential. Now retired and back in Norfolk, living with her husband Marcus and dog Basil, she has decided to try her hand at creative writing.

M.C. Gardner has written poems, prose and has translated from English and French poetry.

She became part of Exiled Writers Ink/ Voices in a Strange Land Biannual Poetry Project (www.exiledwriters.co.uk) who published her Poems in 2009, and her short story 5th March 1953 in Exiled Writers Ink magazine in 2010, and invited her to read poetry at The Poetry Society UK/ Poetry Café (07-02-2011). Her poems have been published in OU Poetry Society Openings annual anthology 25/2008 – 33/2016. Éditions Poètes à vos plumes (Paris 2016), has published her poetry.

The UEA 140 story project www.miniaturestory.org/authors/included her miniature stories in 2014, 2015, and 2016.

Cynthia Gallogo wants to save the world with her involvement in international causes for disadvantaged children, women and families. Now, she is a full-time mum, and is saving herself first and her family, one day at a time. Recruited from her home country as a social worker, she has worked for Save the Children, Norfolk County Council and an Independent Fostering Agency. When she's not working, she's challenging herself to learn new things, be it cooking, gardening, playing a new musical instrument, writing, or spending time with friends.

Jan Godfrey MBE is a 'Waylander' through and through, having lived in Carbrooke for almost all of her very long life. While loving the rural way of life, and the amazing Wayland environment, she battles for better facilities, especially for the young. She spends a great deal of her time writing, which she mostly loves, but 'life-writing' has given her a wonderful opportunity for reflection.

Belona Greenwood is founder and co-organiser of Words and Women working alongside Lynne Bryan. A former journalist she took an MA in Scriptwriting at the University of East Anglia and writes plays for adults and children, produced and performed both regionally and nationally. She is co-director of Chalk Circle Theatre Company. In 2009 she was a winner of the Decibel Penguin Prize for Life Writing, and she has won an Escalator award to write a book of creative non-fiction. She teaches adults and children.

Hilary Hanbury:

Age – irrelevant but drawing my pension.

Happily divorced from short term partner.

Encouraged to write at an early age by my mother who entered my first attempt at age nine into a national competition run by Cadbury's Chocolate. I won, to my family's amazement, and we lived on chocolate for a year. The bigger prize was the certificate which I still have on my wall to this day reminding me that all is within grasp. I have three lovely daughters and four grandchildren. I still love writing and recently rediscovered poetry.

Jenni Jones is a pseudonym

Julia Howarth was born in High Peak, Derbyshire in 1945: Happy childhood, books, drawing, walking, visits to New Mills Library, walking! Early reader, taught by mum. Between walks, a "naughty baby" serial about my brother and other stories. Wonderful varied nursing career, A&E sister, District Nursing in Salford, (walking) and Norfolk in CAR!! Happily retired in Swaffham, still love books, writing poems and prose. Married, 4 children, 4 stepchildren, 14 grandchildren. Still walking, (more slowly).

Nichola Lovell: I grew up on USAF bases around the world. Somehow I've found myself settled in Norfolk. I've become accustomed to country walks and eating fish & chips by the North Sea. I enjoy traveling, deep conversation and anything mysterious. I am an eclectic reader with a passion for horror-fiction and fantasy. At the age of 15, I discovered Stephen King and have felt inspired to write ever since.

Lyn Mckinney: Born in Worthing, Sussex in 1951. Most of her working career has been with the BBC, with a little Anglia TV thrown in. Married Jimmy, TV director, in London and moved to Norfolk in 1975 for 2 years. Two children and 42 years later, still in the same house. Retired in 2011 as a News Producer for BBC Radio Norfolk. Deep love for animals, the sea, theatre and the arts, and has always wanted to write creatively.

Rhonda Peak: Originally from Derbyshire, Rhonda is a charity administrator who lives in Swaffham, Norfolk, with her husband and two young children. Her main hobbies are singing in a rock choir, eating gingerbread and riding her unicycle. She is yet to master doing all three at the same time.

Maxine Robertson loves getting inside other people's heads and is rapidly approaching the end of her counselling training. In the hope of preventing herself from seizing up completely, she regularly attends pilates classes. The main members of her fan club include a Scottish husband, a daughter, a bouncy Jack Russell (Alfie), five very spoiled cats and two ancient hens. Other interests include books, wildlife and, of course, creative writing.

Jane Rudd loves living by the sea and has spent most of her life in Gorleston-on-Sea. She is new to creative writing and has found inspiration from childhood memories and observing people around her. She has many interests among them spending time with family, swimming, yoga and walking in the fresh air.

Leah Spencer nee Cartman:

1940s I am born on Merseyside to Eileen and Tom, who are glad to be alive.

1950s I am in North Wales, the oldest of 4 children and go to school, where I am quiet and compliant, yet can still get caned for giggling.

1960s I see the Beatles at Llandudno; swap my small town existence for the bright lights of Liverpool; buy my first mascara; become a teacher and marry Philip.

1970s Brief escape south to Somerset and Bath, where our son David is born. We move back to Liverpool and then to Swaffham, where I buy wellies and join the WI. (Am I the only WI member to sing Jerusalem in the Albert Hall and scream to the music of Ian Drury and the Blockheads at the UEA in the same week?)

1980s Move to Beachamwell, a lovely village, where we have lived ever since. Become head teacher of a tiny village school and enjoy pre-National Curriculum bliss!

1990s I move to a bigger school, the National Curriculum and Ofsted inspections … what joy! David marries Ellie and they settle in Norfolk.

2000s I start acting at Westacre; retire from teaching and discover printing, quilting and creative writing.

2010s With so much still to do – I am really hoping that 2016 will prove that 70 is the new 60 …

Jurgita Stipiniene:

You cannot find me in any supermarket or jewellery store!

Meet me – washed up from overseas, a rare and unique diamond with lots of imperfections, not very clear but every corner has been polished by sometimes joyful, sometimes stormy but never boring life experiences. I have learned that every person or circumstance I have ever met in my life has either made me sparkle less or shine brighter!

Sometimes, instead of shining like a diamond, I like to be a pebble and I try to collect every ray of sunshine and fill myself with light, happiness, wisdom and joy so that I can share this with others.

I've been blessed with the opportunity to expand – I have two unique – in every sense – little diamonds. They are precious and I love them.

Katrina Stockdale: I'm 66 years old and I am the oldest living artefact in our local museum. I love anything about history and going around stately houses and museums.

Heidi Williamson is a poet, tutor, and writing coach. She's worked in schools, museums, private companies and as a writer-in-residence. She studied poetry and prose at the UEA, and reads and delivers workshops regularly throughout the UK. Her first collection Electric Shadow (Bloodaxe, 2011) was a Poetry Book Society Recommendation and shortlisted for the Seamus Heaney Centre Prize for Poetry. The Print Museum, her next collection, was published by Bloodaxe in March, 2016.

Jayne Winterbone is proud to be Norfolk born and bred, although she has been known to sneak across the border in search of adventure, real ale, cream teas and anyone who can pronounce her surname correctly. Jayne teaches yoga and loves riding her motorbike, although sadly not at the same time. She lives in deepest Breckland, in a fairy cottage in an enchanted garden with a hairy woodwose (woodlouse) and an assortment of wildlife to keep her company.

Lightning Source UK Ltd.
Milton Keynes UK
UKOW05f0732191016

285627UK00007B/71/P

9 781910 061411